Baptists and the American Tradition

BAPTISTS
AND THE
AMERICAN
TRADITION

Robert C. Newman

To John LineBerry ~ A Co-worker in Christ,

Bob Newman

Heb. 13:2

To Betty,
my helpmeet in the gospel.

Contents

Preface

I can lay no claim to originality. This book, like most, is the product of numerous impressions from many sources. Space will not permit a complete listing of appreciation, but I would like to mention six persons among the many.

I extend thanks to Rev. Douglas E. Christen, my spiritual "Paul" who first introduced me to the Baptist position soon after conversion. Of my many mentors over the years, two have been most helpful regarding the content of this volume. I mention Professor Howard Washburn since he first introduced me to Baptist history. To Professor Earle E. Cairns I owe an immense debt for placing before me the whole vista of American religious history with its underlying uniqueness. To Rev. Floyd D. Drake, Book Editor of Regular Baptist Press, I am grateful for his willingness to publish this fledgling effort. To Mrs. William Johnstone I give my many thanks for hours spent in patient typing of the manuscript. My gratitude is also extended to Miss Beth Soderstrom for grammatical corrections. Any mistakes in grammar or historical accuracy may be laid at my door.

A word to my readers with regard to aim. I have attempted middle ground and have written for a general audience, both Baptist and non-Baptist. By means of footnoting and bibliography, I have sought to provide the student and the scholar with helps to deeper source materials on the subject.

One final note concerns itself with changing definitions and impressions. I would caution the reader to keep foremost in mind that I have used the word "dissent" in its colonial context. The early Baptist dissenters share little in common with what frequently passes for dissent in our generation. Twentieth-century rebellion is often a dissent without moral rooting. The early Baptists, on the other hand, were dissenters who had a firm grip on eternal things in the Bible. Their dissent was meaningful because of this firm Biblical mooring. They did not advocate the immoral or an anarchy bred out of a cry for freedom without responsibility. We all owe them a great debt.

Introduction

What is told in the following pages is the story of persecution. But it is more than just persecution. It is also the story of the dissent which caused it. By dissent we mean religious dissent— very strong religious dissent with an uncompromising and unrelenting spirit. Dissent and the resulting persecution usually produce reaction and change. Our story is not only concerned with the dissent and persecution, but with what this produced by way of lasting change.

Even the casual observer of the American scene is aware that religiously the United States is unique. But beyond some vague and often mistaken notions he cannot tell why America has a religious heritage quite unlike that of its European counterparts. The reasons are many and varied. We shall not pursue every facet of American religious history. That has been frequently and ably accomplished by writers and scholars.

What we intend to do is to extract from the history of one body of religious America enough of its heritage to establish a premise and reach a conclusion. The premise, quite simply stated, is that, to a large degree, America is what it is in religious pursuit because of Baptist dissent. To put it another way, the early dissent of the Baptists of colonial America helped to forge and shape the American religious tradition, a tradition wondered at and envied by many world religious observers. Thus, our conclusion will be to assess the legacy left by the Baptists to the American religious tradition because they were willing and even eager for dissent. The story is not a new one. It has often been related in many volumes dealing with colonial American religious history. What has not been done is to center on the theme of the Baptist legacy to the American tradition by highlighting their outstanding forefathers and how their dissent helped to mold our religious heritage. Note should be taken concerning the method of approach. The ensuing pages are not a colonial Baptist history. Quite the contrary, they simply extract from that history certain persons and related events in an attempt to reconstruct a pattern of dissent, persecution, change and legacy. On the face of it, this involves some decision making, and some readers may feel it to be arbitrary in method. After all, did not all early Baptists contribute to the cause? No doubt they did to some degree, at least those in positions of leadership. Yet choices have to be made or our tale of Baptist influence in the forming of the American tradition would bog down in a mire of minute detail. In an effort to avoid the above, the writer highlights the work of four early Baptist leaders—Roger Williams (1603-1683), John Clarke (1609-1676), Isaac Backus (1724-1806) and John Leland (1754-1841). From these dates in history it can be observed that they fall into a somewhat chronological sequence of early America. Williams and Clarke serve to highlight the early beginnings. Backus exerted his influence during the Great Awakening and the American Revolution. Leland figures prominently in the revolutionary and disestablishment period. These four also represent the two geographic areas of colonial and revolutionary America where Baptist influence and persecution were keenest, namely Rhode Island and Virginia. The reader will discover other names and leaders in the text, but these four were the essential molders of the Baptist heritage.

A word should be said concerning non-Baptist dissent. Baptists were not alone in objecting to the religious inequities of early America. The Quakers endured as much, and sometimes more, opposition and persecution. Presbyterians came in for their share, as did the Anglicans in New England and, to some extent, others as well. The aim is not to minimize the impact of other groups to the cause of the American religious tradition. The purpose is to relate the contributions of one of several bodies.

The reader may ask, "What do you mean by the American

religious tradition?" In answer we propose the following: First, the separation of church and state. By this is meant the separation of powers, not isolation from individual Christian influence. Second, the rise of American religious pluralism, or the flourishing of many religious bodies with an openly competitive spirit. Third and finally, the spirit of voluntarism. This unique facet of the American religious scene has to do with the freedom of Americans to do what they wish religiously, thus creating church growth and evangelism through propagation rather than through legislation or coercion.

Since the purpose of this study is to present the Baptist influence in the forming of the American religious tradition, we begin with the date of 1606 and end with 1833. The former date represents the founding of Virginia and precedes the landing of the Plymouth Puritan Separatists, allowing us to trace the background of the rebellion which created Rhode Island, that colony of "the otherwise-minded." The latter entry of 1833 figures as the year when the Massachusetts legislature disestablished the Congregational Church by means of a constitutional amendment. Between these two dates our story unfolds.

One
The Background of Dissent

Gospel and Gold

Many have suggested a pursuit of gold populated Central and South America while a pursuit of God prodded the early settlers of North America. It was really more complex. To be sure, the southern part of the western hemisphere found the Spanish, Portuguese and others lusting for riches. Yet their Anglo-Saxon counterparts in eastern North America were not "Simon-pure" in their rationale for colonization. It can, however, be generalized that whereas in Central and South America they took their church with them, in North America they intended to plant one. Many colonists were not on a religious quest, but in a large percentage of cases the leadership was.

The early colonizing attempt by Gilbert and Raleigh can be classified as a washout, the whole colony having vanished without a trace. By 1606 another effort brought meager but certain success. The Virginia Company began a settlement and English colonization was underway. Of the several reasons for this effort our two above suggestions were both present. Gold came first and

God came second, in that order. It was a joint-stock company with the shareholders expecting a return on their investment. Admittedly, there was also a desire to convert the Indians. Tobacco raising rescued the enterprise from otherwise certain financial disaster, but the death toll for the little colony was grim during the first few years. Gaustad points to some discernable religious motives for the founding of Virginia based upon the wording of the Royal Charter dated April 10, 1606.[1] The growth of the Anglican Church in Virginia was slow and painful but destined to control religious matters in the settlement for many years. By 1624 Virginia had become a royal colony with the Anglican Church the sole religious body.

Other colonies followed suit between 1620 and 1733. In all, there were actually sixteen, with Virginia opening the door. Plymouth followed in 1620 and Georgia ended with Oglethorpe opening his "debtor's jail" in 1733. Various maneuvers and mergers among the sixteen colonies gradually reduced their number to what became before 1775 the "original thirteen colonies."

Experiments in Toleration

Religious motives can be discovered as a factor in nearly all of these early plantings, vying always with business interests. However, some form of the old world church-state union, in the practical colonial expression, held sway in all colonies except Maryland, Rhode Island and Pennsylvania, where experiments in church-state separation and religious freedom were the order of the day.

In Maryland the reason was practical. Cecilius Calvert (Lord Baltimore) began his colony for profit and a haven for his fellow English Catholics. Only a small number fled to his refuge so a door was opened to religious toleration by means of a legislative act in 1649 which provided religious liberty to all but atheists, Unitarians and Jews.[2] Lord Baltimore hoped to attract Protestants in

1. Edwin Scott Gaustad, *A Religious History of America*, p. 38.
2. H. Shelton Smith, Robert T. Handy and Lefferts A. Loetscher, *American Christianity*, Vol. 1, pp. 35-39.

order to sustain an economic base. Indeed, he did attract them. They grew so strong that in 1654 an act was passed withdrawing toleration toward the Roman Catholics in Maryland.[3] The Protestants then pushed for the establishment of the Anglican Church, an event occurring by 1702.

Since the Rhode Island Experiment in religious freedom is one of the chief interests of this volume, we simply note here that it was one of three colonial attempts in liberty, and move quickly to "Penn's Woods." William Penn (1644-1718), London-born, was an ardent follower of George Fox and his Quaker movement. Expelled in 1661 from Christ Church, Oxford, for his Nonconformist views, he served briefly in the English Navy and studied law in London. Penn was imprisoned several times for his nonconformity. These occasions allowed time for writing. After his marriage in 1672, he helped eight hundred Quakers secure a footing in New Jersey (1677-78).

In 1681 Penn obtained a proprietary charter for settlement of Pennsylvania from Charles II. The king owed his father a debt and the ensuing charter for Pennsylvania was the payment. Penn's Pennsylvania settlement became his "Holy Experiment," and his *Frame of Government* (1682) was the articulation of his political policies which included religious tolerance and fair treatment of the Indians. Like all of the Middle Colonies—New York, New Jersey, Pennsylvania, and Delaware—"Penn's Woods" enjoyed the immigration of a variety of Europeans, each with its own culture and religious heritage. Especially in Pennsylvania the atmosphere was conducive to religious liberty.

Penn was also a businessman. By application of good marketing and advertising, he got his experiment moving. By the 1690s the population boasted several thousand, with a large sprinkling of Quakers from New England, England and New Jersey (an early Quaker haven), as well as a good smattering of other sects and groups. Penn guaranteed religious liberty to all except atheists. Pressures from London later forced him to restrict officeholding

3. Ibid., p. 40.

from Roman Catholics. He died in 1718 a broken man. The accumulation of various troubles within his colony, with the English crown and with finances, including time in debtor's prison, impaired his health and hastened his death. His colony proved a success, however, and Pennsylvania became a veritable tapestry of religious pluralism with numerous Quakers, Lutherans, Presbyterians, Baptists and others.

Plymouth—A New Church Begun

"The Lord hath more truth and light yet to break forth out of His holy Word." These sentiments of John Robinson, pastor to the Pilgrims during their temporary religious asylum in Holland, highlight the thinking of these English Puritan Separatists. Why Holland? Quite simply, these English Puritans had fled to Leyden in 1608 due to religious intolerance in England. In their view, the Church of England was heir to the Lutheran Reformation but had not gone far enough. Thus, since the Anglican Church was not yet pure in government, worship or membership, the only open recourse was to begin anew. To purify within was no longer an option. England did not miss them—the Separatists were seldom missed. Holland could not be their final home for they were Englishmen.

Therefore, in 1620, the Speedwell and the Mayflower set forth from southern England, the former vessel having first transported the Robinson group from Holland. In England they united with other Puritan Separatists who had elected to join them. After the Speedwell, due to leaks, refused to "speed well," both ships returned to the English port with their passengers. The Mayflower then commenced the historic journey alone with one hundred two aboard. Of these, fewer than half were Separatist Puritans.

Two months, one death and one birth later they arrived just off Cape Cod. This proved a problem since their destination and invitation to settle were in Virginia. Feeling that God had directed by His providence, they began their "Plymouth" colony without charter and thus without legal authority. Their government was simply the *Mayflower Compact.* This agreement, modeled after their church covenant used in Holland, remained their basic legislative instrument until 1691 when Plymouth united with Massachusetts. If gold had prompted other plantings, surely this one can be ascribed to religious intent.

The colony grew slowly, especially since the great English migrations did not occur until 1630 and after. For nine years they were pastorless, Robinson having remained behind with the small remnant in Holland. Religious concerns were in the able hands of one William Brewster, the ruling elder. Their first minister, Ralph Smith, came in 1629. True, his arrival was preceded by John Lyford, an unworthy minister sent by their English partners, the Plymouth Company; but he was promptly expelled. The Church was the center of life in the little colony. Strictness of all matters was the order—an attitude which resulted in few people being attracted to Plymouth. They believed God would have them build a new church, one fully committed to Separatist principles, including a congregational polity, simplicity of worship and a regenerated church membership which was in full control of the political affairs of the settlement.

Massachusetts—Purifying from Afar

By the 1630s the growing persecution under England's archbishop Laud produced "The Great Migration." Gradually, thousands fled to the New World. By 1642 some sixteen thousand Puritans had found refuge in and around Boston; others fled to Virginia and Maine, a few to other colonies and a large number to the islands off Florida, especially St. Kitto and Barbados. These later Puritans in New England settled under the auspices of the Massachusetts Bay Company. Thus, it was again a religious migration with a commercial base. These Boston Puritans were not only greater in number than their brethren in Plymouth, but also different in kind. Like the Plymouth group, they were Calvinists, congregationalists in church government and believers in a strong regenerate church membership—one which would control the political affairs of the colony. They accomplished this by restricting officeholding and voting privileges to the church member, thereby disenfranchising a large portion of the populace. In one respect they differed from Plymouth. They believed in the Anglican way. They simply believed, like Plymouth, that the Reformation was not yet complete. Unlike Plymouth, Boston believed the method was to purify the old from within, not by separation but by completion of the Reformation of the Church of England. What better place to finish than three thousand miles away, away from Laud and the persecution! In sum, the Puritans of Massachusetts Bay were not Separatists, they were simply purists.[4] They had not taken the final step, in theory at least. The Bible Commonwealth was their concept of the best of two worlds—purity of church and purity of government.

Plymouth and Massachusetts were really not so far apart as they had thought, for by 1691 the two colonies merged. In both, the Congregational Church held sway and religion was tolerated only if one went their way. How and why the "New England way" controlled civil and religious affairs and how and why the Baptists resisted is the subject of chapter two.

Reviewing the Early Plantings

To summarize the early colonial background, in all except three colonies some form of a practical church-state union held sway, and religious uniformity was the usual picture. In New England and Virginia it was strongest. Some measure of religious diversity began to creep in by way of the Middle Colonies, due to diversified settlers. For the most part, however, only in three colonies were a large and open degree of religious toleration and church-state separation attempted. In Maryland a good beginning, while begun out of economic rather than religious scruple, soon wasted

---

4. For those interested in understanding the New England Puritans the writer suggests the writings of Perry Miller and his three books: *The New England Mind from Colony to Province, The New England Mind: The Seventeenth Century* and *Orthodoxy in Massachusetts, 1630-1650, A Genetic Study.*

away until the established church was Anglican. Only in Rhode Island and Pennsylvania would an open spirit of toleration, a freedom from religious persecution and a stated and practiced church-state separation be maintained from its founding, on through the Revolution and up to the disestablishment period. This background allows us to view the arrival of the Baptists.

Two
The Early Beginnings of Dissent

The Baptists Arrive

Actually, the Baptists did not truly immigrate, at least not at first. The earliest beginnings in the New World were the result of dissent from the prevailing New England Congregationalism.

Roger Williams must be credited with the first planting of the Baptists. In 1638 a church was formed under his temporary leadership in Providence. There is evidence to support the contention that this was a Baptist church practicing believer's baptism in 1639.[1]

A second dissenters congregation was established in Newport in late 1638 or early 1639 by Dr. John Clarke, a contemporary co-worker of Williams. Disagreements arose and Clarke formed another church along Baptist lines in or before 1644. His first church became a Quaker body. During Clarke's absence in England (1651-1664) his Baptist church suffered two divisions, the first becoming a Six-Principle Baptist movement and the second a Seventh Day Baptist church.

1. John Winthrop, *History of New England,* Vol. 1, pp. 352, 353.

The theology of both Williams and Clarke was Calvinistic, therefore in harmony with New England Puritanism, their former orientation. This was not true of all colonial Baptists. Arminian Baptists were more numerous until 1742, especially in New England.[2] The first Baptist Association was organized in Philadelphia in 1707 with five churches represented. By 1742 they had adopted a Calvinistic confession of faith based upon a London confession of 1689. This turned the tide of opinion toward a more Calvinistic Baptist movement in early America.

Growth was slow for the colonial Baptists in the seventeenth century. In 1660 there were only four congregations, all in Rhode Island, with two in Providence and two in Newport. By the century's end there were something over twenty Baptist churches with Massachusetts and Rhode Island accounting for over half of them. Growth in Pennsylvania began in 1684. German and Welch Baptists immigrated in the late seventeenth and early eighteenth centuries, mainly to the middle colonies. The growth was greatest in this area and Virginia. John Leland reported some one hundred fifty ordained Baptist preachers by 1790.[3] Gaustad notes a total colonial growth from four congregations in 1660 to over four hundred fifty by 1780. The slowest growth was the period of 1660-1680, while advances between 1720 and 1780 rapidly accelerated.[4]

Roger Williams:
The "Windmill in the Low Countries"

Cotton Mather, learned theologian and historian for New England Puritanism, described Williams in his chapter entitled "Little Foxes; or, The Spirit of Rigid Separation in One Remarkable Zealot." Among other things, he likened this agitator to a "certain Windmill in the Low Countries . . . who being a preacher that had less light than fire in him, hath by his own sad example, preached

2. William W. Sweet, *The Story of Religion in America,* p. 76.
3. Edwin Scott Gaustad, *Historical Atlas of Religion in America,* p. 11
4. Ibid., p. 11.

unto us the danger of that evil which the apostle mentions in Romans 10:2."[5]

Williams could agitate! Claimed by the Baptists, he was actually the permanent follower of no one. He was, in turn, an Anglican, a Puritan, a Separatist, a Baptist and a Seeker.

His arrival in history was inconspicuous. He was born in London, the son of James and Alice Williams, sometime between the years 1603-1606. His father was a merchant tailor from a family of business background. His mother came from the family of Pemberton in St. Albans. Roger was London-born and city-reared. The family had grown up under Tudor reign, and like many such families of the day, aspired to gentility. In 1623 he entered Cambridge University's Pembroke College under the recommendation of the jurist Edward Coke who was impressed with the young man. He graduated with his Bachelor's degree in 1627, spending two additional years in graduate study. He left without finishing. Brockunier suggests a reason in that Williams, while at Cambridge, had come under Puritan doctrine and was fast moving toward Separatist principles.[6] Since Archbishop Laud was in control of the Anglican church his fortunes in England were becoming limited.

In 1629 he was episcopally ordained and made chaplain in the household of Sir William Masham. This proved a turning point, for it allowed him to meet one Jane Whalley, with whom he fell in love but did not marry. Disappointed all around, he came into contact with advocates of the Massachusetts Bay Colony enterprise. In December 1629 he married a little-known woman, Mary Barnard. The next year he determined to leave England. On February 5, 1631, he and his wife stepped off the ship *Lyon* in Boston harbor. Along with his wife and baggage he brought a keen mind, an excellent preaching ability, a searching spirit and ideas of church purity that were to rock Massachusetts to the very core.

5. Cotton Mather, *Magnalia Christi Americana;* or, *The Ecclesiastical History of New England*, Vol. 2, p. 495.
6. Samuel Hugh Brockunier, *The Irrepressible Democrat, Roger Williams, p. 23.*

John Clarke: "A livelie experiment . . .
with full liberty in religious concernments"

If Williams was the "Windmill," Clarke was the balance wheel. What Williams formulated, Clarke carried out. Williams' ensuing enterprises would have failed without the capable leadership of John Clarke. Stokes and Pfeffer reflect with great favor upon his much overlooked work in the cause of early American Baptist history and freedom of conscience.[7]

Born in England in 1609, little is known of Clarke's early years. He was of well-to-do parents, and was the sixth offspring in a family of eight children. Clarke married three times—to Elizabeth Harges (died 1671), Jane Fletcher (died 1672) and Sarah Davis, who survived him.

As to his education one can only speculate. Backus reports that he was an ardent student of the Biblical languages.[8] It is known that he was a practicing physician and may have studied at Leyden University in Holland. He composed two works—a concordance-lexicon, and his famous apologetic, *Ill News from New England,* written while Clarke was back in London. This book relates his theology and apologetic against the Massachusetts persecution of dissenting Baptists.

Clarke arrived in Boston and immediately joined with the despised "Antinomians" and "Anabaptists." The former were all those who stressed the Calvinistic Covenant of Grace rather than the Covenant of Works. The latter were various agitators who pushed the Puritan Congregational movement to its logical end. If the Puritans were contending for a regenerate membership based on those who would "own the church covenant," then why not carry the idea to its logical conclusion, namely believer's baptism. These despised groups included extremists like Anne Hutchinson and Samuel Gorton. Clarke could not be described as a fanatic. He

7. Anson Phelps Stokes and Leo Pfeffer, *Church and State in the United States,* pp. 16, 17.
8. Isaac Backus, *A History of New England with Particular Reference to the Denomination of Christians Called Baptists,* Vol. 1, p. 348.

was too even and balanced. He was, however, already a Separatist and would soon embrace Baptist beliefs.

These two men—Williams, the pioneer and visionary, and Clarke, the balance wheel, church leader and statesman—laid the groundwork for what Rhode Island was to become. It was fortunate for both the colony and the Baptists that these two functioned so harmoniously.

The Rhode Island "Way"

Opposing Puritans referred to Rhode Island as little as possible. When they did mention the place it was unaffectionately known as the colony of the "otherwise-minded." Without respect it was known as the "sewer" where God's "debris" had collected and rotted. Their reasons for this attitude centered around its dissenting beginnings.

As soon as Williams arrived in Boston he was gladly received, for "godly ministers," as Winthrop the governor referred to him, were hard to find. Williams soon became hard to dislodge. When Boston's Puritan Congregational church offered him its pulpit he refused. His reason was blunt. He did not wish to pastor an "unseparated people." In Williams' view, Massachusetts, which still considered itself one with the Church of England and simply on an errand of purification in New England, was really a church of Antichrist. He saw their unwillingness to break away as a compromise. In Williams' mind the Puritan "middle way" was not the right way. Saints must be visible. Massachusetts agreed. But saints must also be wholly separate from every taint of compromise. Massachusetts did not agree. At issue was the nature of England's church. With all of its reforming and Puritan elements it clearly was a "mixed multitude," for it was really a national church. In such a setup one became a citizen and a saint simultaneously. In Williams' mind, purification was impossible. The only recourse was to begin anew.

He moved to Salem, hoping for fertile fields. Here the Salemites determined to install him as their pastor. Then Boston took opportunity to take Salem into its confidence, with the result that Salem withdrew its offer to Williams.

Undaunted, he journeyed to Plymouth. Surely here, in Separatist territory, he would find a kindred spirit. After all, the Plymouth saints would find nothing but good in a separatist brother. But he proved a villain even here. Williams contended their church was also "unseparated." But how could this be? First, even though disowning their former affiliation with the Anglican Church, their present church was formed out of it; and with such impure beginnings one could only begin anew. Williams' views of separation were advancing so rapidly that he now found himself out of step with established Separatists. He left Plymouth.

Somehow he was installed as assistant pastor at Salem. He then proceeded to confirm all the previous worst suspicions. He attacked the civil authority. Williams asserted that the magistrates could only punish violators of common decency and various persons who harmed civil laws, and no person ought to be punished for Sabbath-breaking or violating any religious requirement.[9] To add insult to injury, Williams advanced an argument concerning Puritan landholders that made them appear as squatters! The logic was simple. While their charter for Massachusetts was granted by Charles, King of England, it was never his to give since he did not own it. Yes indeed, it belonged to the Indians. A side note at this point is in order. When Williams moved to Providence he bought land from the Narragansett tribe. The author has read the documentation in Bartlett's *Records of Rhode Island.*

The limits of endurance had been reached. Even the noted theologian John Cotton could not silence this dissenter. In 1635 Massachusetts brought Williams to trial and determined that his diverse opinions were not needed. He was summarily exiled. They gave him a bit over a month to get his affairs in order and later extended it to spring. However, all preaching had to stop. But he would not stop; therefore, the civil magistrates determined

9. Gaustad, *A Religious History of America,* pp. 64, 65.

to send him home to England. Williams, getting wind of this, made off into the wilderness in the harsh winter, soon arriving at his "Providence" on the edge of Narragansett Bay. His friends from Salem, his wife and two small children soon joined him.

In 1920 Frederick Jackson Turner, an American historian and proponent of the so-called "Turner Thesis of American History," wrote:

> Western democracy has been from the time of its birth idealistic. The very fact of the wilderness appealed to men as a fair, blank page on which to write a new chapter in the story of man's struggle for a higher type of society. . . . This was the vision that called to Roger Williams.[10]

Williams left, and all was in an uproar. Clarke left, and little was said. This describes the complimentary personalities of the two men. Williams was a gifted preacher, a bold agitator, a visionary and an intellectual. Clarke, on the other hand, was an intellectual with a practical bent, a church planter and quietly consistent.

In 1637 Clarke formed a company of nineteen people. In the winter of 1637-1638 they sallied forth to discover a new home. They traveled first to what is now New Hampshire, then south toward Long Island and Delaware. Stopping on the way at Providence, they ended up staying. Williams and Clarke visited Plymouth to see if they had any claim to the Island of Aquidneck and Sow-wames (Barrington, Rhode Island). Plymouth assured them that the area was open to settlement and appeared reasonably favorable to the idea of having these dissenters as neighbors. Clarke and his followers purchased Aquidneck from the Indians.

Since mention has been made of the early church plantings of both men, we move to civil concerns. On the political side two communities, Newport and Portsmouth, were started on the island. In 1640 they joined to form one government. In 1643 Williams was sent to England under the combined auspices of the Providence and Aquidneck Island people to secure a charter from

10. Frederick Jackson Turner, *The Frontier in American History,* pp. 261, 262.

the government under King Charles I. The colony was herein described as "Providence Plantations, in Narragansett Bay, in New England."[11] His return effected a mixed reaction. Providence heralded it a major achievement. Portsmouth and Newport had objections which were probably due to a desire for complete independence from Providence and possibly spearheaded by a troublemaker named William Coddington. Dissenters produce dissenters! Clarke, though he felt the charter limited, argued for acceptance, and after three years, the independent Baptists on the island agreed. At somewhat the same time he drew up a code of laws to function under the terms of the charter.

From 1647 to 1651 life in the new colony moved along quite reasonably. Williams soon left the Baptists to become a Seeker, but remained in the colony's leadership along with Clarke. He felt no church could be established since the apostles had not succeeded themselves. Neither could a church hold communion nor undertake baptism, this being argued from the same premise. Williams was one of those rare intellectuals willing to carry his point to the ultimate conclusion, even though the conclusion bordered on the absurd.

Clarke, on the other hand, was fully involved not only in colonial leadership but as the pastor of the Newport Baptist Church. In 1651 he, a fellow Baptist preacher named Obadiah Holmes and John Crandall visited one William Witter, an aged member of their church now living, of all places, near Lynn, Massachusetts. Since he had no place of worship and could not travel, the three visited him and conducted a "private" worship service. In the midst of all this the Massachusetts Puritans, apparently privy to what was taking place, sent two constables to the house who then arrested the three men, took them to dinner and then to a Puritan service which was obviously designed to show them the error of their ways. The three men entered, bowed to the assembly, sat down and refused to remove their hats as a sign of contempt for

11. John Russell Bartlett, ed., *Records of the Colony of Rhode Island and Providence Plantations,* Vol 1, p. 145.

their treatment. The men attempted a defensive argument but were silenced.

After the service they were confined in a Boston jail for ten days, then tried and sentenced without witnesses or defense. The charges revealed the Massachusetts intransigent attitude. The men were indicted for holding a "Private Meeting," serving communion to an excommunicated person, rebaptizing converts and other assorted offenses.[12] The three accused men neither admitted nor denied the charges. Clarke and Crandall had their fines paid by unknown friends. Holmes endured a flogging after being incarcerated until September. The whole incident provoked Clarke's *Ill News from New England,* written in London to gain a sympathetic ear from the English Puritans.[13]

Coddington, a "fly in the ointment" who had opposed the union of the islanders with Providence, journeyed to England in 1649 following the death of Charles I. He obtained a commission making him governor of the islands of Aquidneck and Conanicut. It was to be a lifelong arrangement with an advisory council of six men named by the people and appointed by himself. This aroused the populace and caused them to send Williams and Clarke to England. They succeeded in having this commission revoked in 1652. Coddington took it gracefully, order was restored and Coddington was even elected governor in 1674 and 1678. Clarke always declined this position, though he served two times as deputy governor and in other roles.

The importance of relating this colonial activity is to be found in the fact that it took Williams and Clarke to England to strengthen the little settlement's political fortunes. Williams soon left England, but Clarke remained, finally securing a second and final charter (1663), granted under the reign of Charles II. It is significant that Clarke labored in England toward this project for some

---

12. John Clarke, *Ill News From New England,* p. 4. The incident is also covered by Backus, *A History of New England,* pp. 173-212 and Henry Melville King, *A Summer Visit of Three Rhode Islanders.*

13. Unfortunately, the volume is not in print. The writer has a microfilm copy of the book taken from an extant copy in the British Museum.

thirteen years (1651-1664). He worked at it during the turmoil of the Commonwealth government following the execution of Charles I (1649-1653), then during the Protectorate (1653-1660) under Cromwell. He had the charter in hand three years after the restoration of the Crown under Charles II.

This charter, obtained by his able statesmanship and fully endorsed by Williams, was to function as Rhode Island's colonial and state constitution until 1843. Beyond that, it was a document fully establishing religious liberty and freedom of conscience.[14] The charter put it this way:

> And whereas, in their humble addresse, they have freely declared, that it is much on their hearts (if they may be permitted), to hold forth a livelie experiment, that a most flourishing civill state may stand and best bee maintained, and that among our English subjects, with full libertie in religious concernments.[15]

The charter spells out the most liberal policy in civil and religious freedom ever granted the colonies under English control.

Clarke and Williams had succeeded in their "livelie experiment." Sweet, the dean of American church historians, puts it this way: "His colony of Rhode Island was the only one to be established squarely on the principle of the separation of church and state and was the first civil government in the world to achieve complete religious freedom."[16] Williams, the "Windmill," and Clarke, whom we have dubbed the "balance wheel," stand in front of the American religious tradition of church-state separation. Clarke alone stands out as the first consistent Baptist church pioneer.

Testing the Theory

To propose a theory or even to establish one is one matter. To make it work is quite another. Since Rhode Island was so open in

---

14. MacDonald, ed., *Documentary Source Book of American History,* pp. 67, 68.
15. Ibid., p. 68.
16. William W. Sweet, *The Story of Religion in America,* p. 67.

its policies, it attracted the disinherited and disenfranchised from everywhere. First came the case of Samuel Gorton, one of the original settlers. In 1640 he was publicly whipped in Providence. The reason was apparently some sort of plot toward anarchy or insurrection. In this case civil liberty for others was at stake. Later, apparently restored and forgiven, he and his own town of Warwick were both included as vital elements of the final united colony. Rhode Island proved to her critics that dissent from within could be controlled when other people's liberties were threatened.

Next came the religious dissenters from without. In the early days of Rhode Island, perhaps as early as 1658, Jewish immigrants arrived from the Iberian peninsula. These first Hebrew settlers were only the beginning. Jews came from several European countries. Unable to erect a house of worship for over one hundred years, they finally constructed their Touro Synagogue at Newport in 1763. It remains America's oldest surviving Jewish religious building. God's covenant people had found a haven among the Baptists.

The Quaker movement traces its beginnings to England and George Fox (1624-1691). His Society of Friends, as they came to be known, seemed destined to be harassed and snubbed everywhere they went. By 1676 so many had found refuge in the Rhode Island haven that an Anglican missionary suggested they were as strong as the Baptists, or perhaps even stronger.[17] Quakerism was the first of several American sects stressing an "Inner Light" form of mysticism. Williams was all for admitting them, but agreement with their ideas was another question. This provides a most excellent example of the Baptist idea of toleration, although, by this time, Williams had forsaken the Baptists. Yet the principle was there. He agreed, as did Clarke and the rest of the leadership, that the Quakers should be admitted. Williams could not, however, remain silent. When Fox himself arrived in 1672, Williams was ready for debate. He had drawn up fourteen points for the proposed confrontation which never took place. Williams then picked

17. Gaustad, *A Religious History of America,* p. 67.

up his pen and proceeded to give the Quakers a broadside via the printed page. His effort, entitled *George Fox Digged Out of His Burrowes* (Boston, 1676) was answered, in kind, by Fox—*A New England Firebrand Quenched* (London, 1678).

Even the English Anglican movement found refuge in Rhode Island, not being welcomed in the rest of New England. French Huguenots joined the English Anglicans, having fled France's persecution of their kind. Almost humorously, even the New England Congregationalists began to come!

A Theological Base

The function of this chapter has been to relate the early Baptist dissenting tradition in New England. We have also attempted to lay bare the foundations of Rhode Island, the first state of its kind in history to allow complete freedom of conscience for all persons while providing for the common good in civil concerns. In essence, Rhode Island became the incubator of the American religious tradition—that is, church-state separation, religious pluralism and voluntarism. It was years ahead of its time. It also set in motion a principle not yet extinguished in America in over three hundred years. Upon what philosophical or, better yet, upon what theological base did Williams and Clarke build?

It is known, for example, that Williams was a personal friend of John Milton and several English Puritans, many of whom entertained ideas of religious liberty far advanced for the day.[18] Williams wrote widely but his works are hard to understand. He could begin a sentence and, seemingly, never finish it. An example of this is his major publication on the Massachusetts tyranny, *The Bloudy Tenet of Persecution for Cause of Conscience* (1644) and its sequel, *The Bloudy Tenet Yet More Bloudy*.

One small piece of writing has been preserved which fully reveals his scheme and philosophy of religious and civil liberty. It is called his famous "ship" letter. Written in 1652, this brief note by

18. Brockunier, *The Irrepressible Democrat, Roger Williams,* p. 202.

Williams sets forth the analogy of a ship at sea. All within the vessel represent a "commonwealth." Sometimes there are "both papists and protestants, Jews and Turks, ... embarked in one ship." To Williams, the analogy presents three truths respecting religious pluralism in one society. First, he distinguished between the ship's prayer and worship and the ship's course and law enforcement. This is the distinction between the sacred and the secular. Second, Williams declares that the ship's authority may force obedience in the realm of the secular but not in the realm of the sacred. Third, and finally, when the welfare of the commonwealth as a whole is at stake, religious conviction is not a just cause for refusing to obey the lawful demands of the state.[19]

The writing of John Clarke provides us with the theological basis for the above political philosophy. In his *Ill News* Clarke argued cogently against the Massachusetts Puritan method of binding the citizenry to both tables of the law of Moses. This had to do with the "sword of the Spirit" and the "sword of the magistrate." In at least two documents the Puritan divines maintained uniformity and conformity in religious matters.

The Westminster Confession elaborated a case for freedom of conscience and then proceeded to restrict such freedom on the basis of censuring those who are for "publishing of such opinions, or maintaining of such practices, as are contrary to the light of nature, or to known principles of Christianity, whether concerning faith, worship, or conversation."[20]

The Cambridge Platform argued, in similar fashion, that it was the civil magistrate's duty to take care of the "matters of religion, and to improve his civil authority" so that he maintained the populace's "observing of the duties" of both "tables of the law."[21] The first half of the Ten Commandments reflect duty toward God, whereas the second half reflect duty toward our fellow man. The

19. Anson Phelps Stokes and Leo Pfeffer, *Church and State in the United States,* pp. 15, 16.
20. Philip Schaff, *The Creeds of Christendom,* pp. 644, 645.
21. *The Cambridge Platform* in *Readings in the History of Christian Thought,* ed. by Robert L. Ferm, p. 604.

New England leadership, therefore, compelled outward conformity in church worship as well as in such areas as stealing, adultery and killing.

Against this, Clarke urged that care be taken to distinguish between the "two administrations of Christ's power here on earth." He maintained that one of these powers cannot be conferred on other men except through the "two-edged sword of that Spirit." In other words, the only way to enforce conformity in Christian worship is by means of preaching. To urge men to obey God by free and open preaching was, in Clarke's mind, the Biblical method. To compel men to accept Christian truth through civil authority was not taught in the Bible. He went on to say "no believer, or Servant of Christ Jesus" had any authority or liberty to force or constrain men in matters of "conscience" or "worship of his God."[22]

Both Williams and Clarke realized this involved an element of risk. One could be a Baptist in Rhode Island but one could also be a Quaker, a Jew, a Huguenot or even an atheist. In time, all these were to be found within the colony. Eventually, though many years removed from Rhode Island's experiment, all these elements would be present even in Massachusetts. Rhode Island was the incubator, Williams and Clarke the husbandmen.

Unrelenting Massachusetts

In the meanwhile, between the beginning of the Rhode Island experiment and the move to disestablish the Congregational Church in New England, nonconformity would still be sorely prosecuted in all but the Baptist haven.

Examples are many. Two are in order. In 1664 one Thomas Painter of Hingham, Massachusetts, refused to present his child for baptism, after which refusal he was publicly whipped. Henry Dunster, first president of newly established Harvard College, had refused a child for infant baptism in 1654. He was forced to

22. Clarke, *Ill News from New England,* pagination missing.

leave the presidency. This would probably have ended the matter except for his insistent conviction that he be heard on his objections to infant baptism. He disturbed the Cambridge church worship service to set forth his views on the subject. For this act he was tried, judged and compelled to receive an admonition from the Massachusetts General Court. The episode ended with Dunster forced into a semiretirement position as the pastor of a church at Scituate in the more tolerant Plymouth colony.[23]

There were other protests and other dissenters in opposition to the Puritan establishment, but these serve to illustrate that the issue did not die with the departure of Williams and Clarke.

23. Henry C. Vedder, *A Short History of the Baptists,* p. 298.

Three
The Progress of Dissent: New England

Small Advances

Pressures upon the New England Bible commonwealth forced gradual changes in their peculiar form of church-state union. Civil magistrates continued to enforce both "tables of the law," which meant the regulations of the religious as well as the civil life of the populace. The magistrates were considered the "nursing fathers to the church," and as such, they could pass and enforce legislation for tax support of Congregationalism. They could not alter the church's beliefs and worship, a hated memory of the old days in England. But taxation for church support and the trial of heretics were within their domain. Not until 1728 did Puritan New England exempt Baptists, Anglicans and Quakers from taxation for support of the "Standing Order."

In 1689 the English Toleration Act was passed. This legislation permitted the three above-mentioned sects a degree of freedom in worship. In 1692 Massachusetts wrote into its charter the phrase "liberty of conscience." Slowly, but grudgingly, the established order was giving way. Anglicans, Baptists and Quakers (but no one else) had won some concessions. They were tolerated but not appreciated. The Anglicans reminded the Puritans of what they had escaped. The Baptists and the Quakers reminded them of what they wished to avoid.

Matters of change also occurred within Congregationalism. The early colonial leadership had stressed a regenerate membership. This was conceived in the following way. First, infant baptism established a degree of covenantal relationship. Next, there were the privileges of the visible church, especially communion. Lastly and most importantly, the church member had to "own the covenant;" that is, he must acknowledge a conversion to Christ. They conceived a Bible commonwealth in which all the citizens were saved and, therefore, were not only church members but "good men" in society. From the beginning it really did not work. Far too many early settlers were without membership in the church. Needless to say, they were also without many civil rights.

In time, matters grew so deplorable that Solomon Stoddard (1643-1729), an earnest clergyman of Massachusetts and grandfather of Jonathan Edwards, with some others proposed the Half-Way Covenant. Simply stated, it provided that any person could join the parish church if they would at least sign the church covenant (a membership contract), profess a belief in Calvinistic doctrine and live an upright, moral life. These people were allowed "halfway" into the church's membership. They could present their children for baptism but could not take communion or vote on church matters. It allowed them a degree of participation in both church and community affairs. It was hoped that these concessions would create a desire for genuine conversion. This proposition began to function in 1662. For the most part it did not succeed in its original intention. People joined under its provision but remained unconverted.

The Great Awakening

The spiritual climate in New England had reached a low ebb by the early 1700s. The Great Awakening provided the answer to this need. Earle Cairns has called this movement "an international Teutonic nonsectarian revival."[1] In Germany it came through the ministry of Philip Spener (1635-1705). It manifested itself in England under the Wesley brothers and George Whitefield. In New England the leader was Jonathan Edwards (1703-1758). In the middle colonies leading lights were the Dutch pastor Frelinghuysen and the Presbyterian William Tennant. It spread to the southern colonies mostly through the efforts of the Methodists.

The Great Awakening was an unusual religious revival, judged by modern standards. First of all, it was not humanly planned. It seems to have arisen almost simultaneously in the various areas mentioned above. Further, it came at a time of great spiritual crisis. Finally, it met a need, especially in North America, by providing a personal and individualized Christian message for those pioneering on the frontier. For our purposes, it can be asserted that the Baptists were one of the groups most benefited by the efforts of the Great Awakening.

Isaac Backus:
"A Door Opened for Equal Christian Liberty"

Isaac Backus (1724-1806) was a product of this revival. Born of a successful and prominent farm family in Norwich, Connecticut, he grew up in a community where religion centered around the Congregational Church. Puritan pioneers from Massachusetts moved to the region in 1635. By 1662 Connecticut had its charter. Religious affairs were quite similar to those in Massachusetts.

The Backus family was neither more nor less religious than the average New England family of that period. In 1740 Backus' father died, leaving his widow with sufficient resources but burdened with eleven children, including a six-week-old infant. Mrs. Backus entered a state of depression from which she recovered through the influences of the Great Awakening.

Isaac's mother had frequently spoken of a religious experience

1. Earle E. Cairns, *Christianity in the United States,* p. 49. Copyright 1964, Moody Press, Moody Bible Institute, Chicago. Used by permission.

occurring to her in 1721. His father became a communicant in the Congregational Church in 1736. Isaac was baptized in the church and regularly attended. As early as 1740 George Whitefield was preaching his revival sermons in New England. The Great Awakening had begun earlier in Edwards' church in Northampton, Massachusetts. The Norwich pastor, Benjamin Lord, was sympathetic toward the movement. He invited several itinerant revivalists to preach in his pulpit. While Whitefield never preached in Norwich, Eleazer Wheelock, Benjamin Pomeroy and James Davenport—all outstanding revivalists of the period—came to exhort the flock. Genuine assurance of salvation came to a number, including the widow Backus. In August of 1741 her son Isaac was converted while working alone in the fields and contemplating the Scriptures and the ministry of the revivalists.

In 1742 Backus became a full-fledged member of the First Congregational Church of Norwich. By this time controversy over the Awakening had started. Those in favor became known as the "New Lights." Those opposing were dubbed the "Old Lights." Decisive conversion was the issue. The leadership of the Standing Order churches were mainly Old Light, with the venerable Charles Chauncey of the First Congregational Church in Boston becoming the spokesman. Jonathan Edwards, himself a pastor of a Congregational church, was an exception, becoming the outstanding leader of the New Lights.

Backus' pastor, Benjamin Lord, had reversed himself by this time. Formerly favoring the revival as a means of awakening a sleeping flock, he now feared what he considered the uneducated and fanatical itinerant preachers. They went from parish to parish and even exhorted the New Light followers in meetings in private homes and barns. The Connecticut legislature passed a law in 1742, at the insistence of the Congregational pastors, which forbade anyone to preach in a parish unless permitted to do so by the established minister. This only served to widen the rift dividing the two sides.

The New Lights were convinced of apostasy and error within the ranks of the Standing Order clergy. In a way, they desired a return to the early days when a regenerate membership was called for by the establishment. They now viewed the Standing Order clergy as both opposers of true faith and the enemies of God. The Old Lights, for their part, were now convinced that chaos had come to rest in New England. The "Separates," as the New Lights became known, were denounced as fanatics. In a strange way it really took on the form of a battle between the educated and the uneducated ministry. There were some exceptions. Edwards, a Yale graduate, and Whitefield, an Oxford scholar, were both pro-revival. Many of their converts, however, became itinerant revivalists. Few of these had much formal training. The Standing Order clergy were well educated and, almost to a man, opposed to the revival by this time.

The New Lights began to separate and form their own churches. McLoughlin points to one hundred twenty-five church separations in New England during the Great Awakening. He further notes that by 1752 a majority of the citizens of Norwich were more sympathetic toward Elder Hide of the Separatist church than toward Pastor Lord.[2] Isaac Backus, his mother and several in his family joined the Separatist church located on Bean Hill near the Backus farm.

In September of 1746 Backus delivered his first sermon, thus testing and confirming his "gift" of preaching. This launched his career as the outstanding spokesman of the day for New Light "Pietism." He began an itinerant preaching ministry and eventually undertook a trip with Elder Joseph Snow of Providence. Their journey carried them to a parish in Massachusetts called Titicut, a place filled with New Light advocates. The moderates and radicals had been unable to agree on a pastor, but when Backus arrived his preaching stirred the radicals to the point of asking him to remain as their leader. The moderates became his enemies. In February of 1748 a Separatist church was established with sixteen members. On April 13, 1748, they ordained Backus as pastor with the aid of

2. Isaac Backus, *Isaac Backus on Church, State and Calvinism, Pamphlets, 1754-1789,* ed. by William G. McLoughlin, pp. 4, 5.

Separatists from Connecticut and Rhode Island.

In the same year the supporters of the established order came out with a tax to complete the parish meeting house. Backus and the Separates were duly billed. He refused to pay his share which was five pounds. For this he was threatened with jail. A friend paid the sum and the authorities let Backus go. Others in the church were less fortunate. Several had their goods sold at auction and one woman remained in jail for thirteen months.[3] The die was cast. Such persecution made Backus determined to fight the system to the end. He began to devleop a theory of church-state separation with far-flung consequences.

The Separatists, however, began to slide toward decline. Two reasons appear as major factors. First of all the "double taxation" system hurt them financially. To maintain their own churches they began voluntary contributions. By means of a religious tax administered by local governments they were forced to maintain the established church, though this ran counter to earlier liberties granted the Baptists, Anglicans and Quakers. The establishment justified the taxation of the Separates on the grounds of their being, in essence, still part of the parish.

The second reason for decline was theological. Like the Rhode Islanders of the previous century, these Separatists now began to question the established church's doctrine of baptism. At first the Separates had simply carried this over to their own church. But in reading the Bible with a literal approach they began to question infant baptism. Controversy arose concerning this issue and hurt the movement.

Two members of Backus' church argued for dropping infant baptism based on two points. First, the Bible clearly did not teach it; and second, both Connecticut and Massachusetts law permitted the Baptists an exemption from paying the tax levied for the maintenance of the established church. His church did not make any immediate decision on the matter.

Backus spent six years studying the question. He wondered

3. Ibid., p. 7.

about the sincerity of those who argued against infant baptism on grounds of avoiding persecution. More importantly, he began to move toward the Baptist concept of a regenerated membership. Even in the early days when Congregationalism had pushed for this concept, it was based on a covenantal relationship. Children baptized of "covenanted" parents were themselves within the covenant. The Puritans believed that God would save the children of parents who were visible saints.

As time went on the Congregational church began to blur the line between converted parents who really "owned the covenant" and those who simply paid lip service and were moral. The Great Awakening highlighted this distinction; in fact, so much so that the Separatists argued, like the Baptists, that only genuinely converted people were proper subjects for church membership. As Backus phrased it, "regenerate souls are the only materials for particular churches."[4] On top of this, it became very difficult to establish how far the "seed" of the covenant extended. Children of converted parents had always been granted baptism and, beginning with the Half-Way Covenant (1662) even the grandchildren of converted parents were entitled to this visible sign.

Backus Turns Baptist

The upshot of all this, so far as Backus was concerned, was quite simple. He preached a sermon in August of 1748 repudiating infant baptism. To later prove his determination, he was immersed on August 22, 1751. He had also married a Baptist woman, one Susanna Mason of Rehoboth, a fact which caused some of his opponents to suggest a confusion in his mind between matters of matrimony and faith. McLoughlin argues that this had little ground for support.[5]

At first Backus practiced open communion, allowing pedo-

4. Backus, *History of New England,* Vol. 2, p. 232.
5. Backus, *Isaac Backus on Church, State and Calvinism,* ed. by William McLoughlin, p. 9.

baptists (infant baptizers) to partake with immersionists. He eventually moved to closed communion, dissolved his church at Titicut and organized the First Baptist Church in Middleborough which functioned as a closed communion body. He never wavered from this final position. This church reordained him.

In 1750 there were somewhat over fifty Baptist churches in all of New England with a large number of them being in Rhode Island.[6] They had as many disagreements as agreements. Most of the Rhode Islanders were Six-Principle Baptists who formed a group known as the General Association. They were Arminians, practicing laying on of hands and rigorously opposing the Calvinistic doctrine of particular election.

A few Rhode Island Baptists worshiped on Saturday (Seventh Day Baptists) and they shunned the Six-Principle Baptist group. In addition, there were a number of Calvinistic Baptist churches. Between 1731 and 1756 six churches in Connecticut and Massachusetts were formed and became known as Five-Principle Particular Baptist Churches. They were still Calvinists, disagreeing with all the rest. Finally, there were Baptists in Rhode Island, Connecticut and Massachusetts who had formed their own Calvinistic association with the added laying-on-of-hands principle.

The Baptists Close Ranks

The ability of Backus as a leader now came to the forefront. He set out to regroup all these Baptists, and to a large degree, he was successful. He persuaded the Old Light people to join ranks with the New Lights. The New Light group consisted of the Backus Separatists lately become Baptists. The Old Lighters were in existence beginning with Rhode Island's infancy. They were pre-Awakening Baptists. They had been stubbornly opposed to the Great Awakening for two reasons. First, they were Arminians whereas the Great Awakening was essentially a Calvinistic movement, particularly in New England. In the second place, they dis-

6. Gaustad, *Historical Atlas,* p. 11.

liked the leadership of the Awakening since it came from the church of their former tormentors.

From 1770 Backus became a leader in knitting together these various factions. In this he was aided by the Warren Baptist Association, which was formed under the leadership of James Manning in 1767. Rhode Island College (Brown University) had already been formed in 1764. The Philadelphia Baptist Association provided the impetus in the creation of both the College and the Warren Association. The Philadelphia fellowship consisted of most of the Baptist churches in Pennsylvania, New Jersey and New York. James Manning, a Baptist graduate from the College of New Jersey (Princeton), became the first president of Rhode Island College.

The fledgling institution provided an educated clergy, thus overcoming the prejudice against Baptists on the part of Congregationalists, who thought them unlearned. Backus became a trustee and served thirty-five years. He also contributed to the school and persuaded the more rural Baptists that Rhode Island College would not turn out the "godless" pastors that came from Harvard and Yale.

The Warren Association proved even more beneficial. In uniting the Baptists it helped them to grow. First, they began to take advantage of the fruits of the Great Awakening. Their simple form of congregational democracy appealed to many of the revival converts. Then, too, it established a more solid theological unity among Baptists. All member churches were required to sign a strict Calvinistic doctrinal statement. They met in annual sessions which proved beneficial in ironing out problems. Of interest at this point is the matter of Backus' first reaction to his church joining the Association. Being a strong Baptist and an independent, he took care to ascertain beforehand whether or not the Association would wield any control over his local congregation. Not until 1770 was he convinced that the Warren Association would not do what the established church had done following the Saybrook Platform of 1708. Using this tool the Congregationalists had permitted ministerial associations to appoint and dismiss pastors and to determine civil action cases with the backing of the magistrates.

The Grievance Committee

In 1769 the Warren Association formed its historic Grievance Committee. Its purpose was to seek "for redress" of grievances related to areas of religious liberty. Its method was the petition system. Over the next number of years this committee, which really amounted to a sort of lobby to seek concessions for religious liberty, performed admirably for the Baptists. In 1769, the same year as its founding, Backus was appointed to its membership although his church was not yet in the Warren Association. Work on this committee allowed him to become a master at petitioning and pamphleteering. Their work was especially effective in Massachusetts. They even appealed, on one occasion, to King George III. This went over the heads of the legislature. So effective was the committee at petitioning all levels of government that, as the Revolution approached, they were accused of disloyalty to the patriot cause. Backus himself had felt that King George and his officials were frequently more sympathetic to the needs of religious liberty than were the patriots.

In 1776 the Association appealed to the First Continental Congress convened in Philadelphia. Backus and Manning, aided by Quakers and Pennsylvania Baptists, drew up a document for religious liberty which they presented to the assembled delegates. McLoughlin relates that John Adams told Backus that any expectation of Massachusetts giving up their established church was doomed to failure.[7]

Backus, however, was no loyalist but a complete patriot. He did not fight, but one son saw action in New England. Backus even preached to the troops, upon occasion. He felt the war had two fronts—one with England and civil liberty and the other with the

---

7. Backus, *Isaac Backus on Church, State and Calvinism,* ed. by William G. McLoughlin, p. 12.

established church and religious liberty.

In 1778 the Grievance Committee petitioned the Massachusetts legislature when they deliberated on a new constitution. Religious taxation was the main issue. Backus was the alert leader in this long controversy. He resorted to newspaper attacks against the proposed constitution for its failure to eliminate taxation to support congregationalism.

Backus died in 1806; but not until 1833 did Massachusetts actually disestablish the Congregational church by removal of the controversial Article Three, though by this time it was essentially a formality. An interesting fact concerning the much disputed Article Three is that it really provided a public tax support of all sects, and the tax was laid upon all. In other words, Backus was a man of principle. He did not simply contest tax support for the established church but tax support of any religious body.

From 1780 to his death Backus was involved in church growth and stability among the Baptists. His *History of New England with Particular Reference to the Denomination of Christians Called Baptists* (1777) is one of the finest documents relating early colonial and Baptist history. It was written at the insistence of his fellow Baptists to set the record straight regarding colonial religious history. They feared the unfavorable writings of the New England Standing Order clergy.

He also advocated a strong Calvinism, especially in the face of rising Arminian thinking among the Baptists. Backus, in a fashion similar to that of Edwards, had slightly modified Calvinism to harmonize more favorably with the fruits of revival, a cause he strongly supported. He had read the English Baptist theologian John Gill who advocated a harsh nonrevival type of Calvinism. Unlike Gill, Backus strongly believed in revivalistic preaching, not feeling it disharmonious with true Calvinism. In a real sense Backus was a figure of theological transition from the lifeless Calvinism of the seventeenth century to the evangelical Calvinism of the eighteenth. He was strong on the sovereignty of God, but not fearful of human effort expended in revival.

A Breach in the Wall

However, our main function at this point is his rationale for church-state separation and religious liberty. Like many others, his thinking evolved from crisis to crisis. At first the issue was practical. When he first became a Separatist, and later a Separatist-Baptist, he simply opposed having to pay taxes to support a church from which he had withdrawn. Later on he began to think more deeply. His first reference point was Scripture. In his famous pamphlet, *A Fish Caught in His Own Net* (1768), Backus frequently quoted the Bible. A certain Reverend Joseph Fish of Stonington, Connecticut, had lost many of his parishioners to the cause of the Separates and Separate-Baptists. Fish and Backus ended up writing and preaching in opposition to one another.

A second source of ideas on religious liberty, as seen in the above-mentioned pamphlet, were the writings of Solomon Paine, Ebenezer Frothingham and Israel Holly. These three were Separatist pedo-baptists. Backus, however, moved beyond them to Baptist ideas. In the pamphlet he describes punishments, imprisonments and other assorted persecutions directed at various Separates and Separate-Baptists on the part of the New England oligarchy.[8] For theological authority he quotes John Owen, John Gill and even Increase Mather. The pamphlet admits the weaknesses of the Separates, such as excessive enthusiasm, lack of education and fanatic attitudes. For historical support he draws upon Thomas Hutchinson's *History of the Colony of Massachusetts Bay* (1764).

Of his several writings we allude to one more. In 1783 he wrote *A Door Opened for Christian Liberty.* It was really a letter written for general circulation among the Baptists in which he urged them to stand firm in their opposition to the passage of the dreaded Article Three of a new Massachusetts constitution. Backus argued, "Religion is ever a matter between God and individuals."[9] The letter also related the persecution of Richard Lee. He con-

8. Ibid., pp. 179-288.
9. Ibid., p. 432.

cluded his letter with seven arguments proving that "God has now set before us an open door for equal Christian liberty which no man can shut."[10] They are as follows:

First, he argued the compact theory of government. The people must consent and support it. From this he insists that one cannot convey to others "things which they have no right to themselves, and no one has any right to judge for others in religious matters."[11] Next, religious taxation has always been imposed by a sect which held all others subordinate to it. Third, Article Three argued that all legislators must acknowledge the Christian religion; but he argued that the Head of the Church is Christ and, since there is no earthly head, then to impose one is unbiblical. Fourth, since the above is true, then a government should not govern in religious affairs. Fifth, the constitution allowed the legislature to make " 'suitable provision' for Christian teachers."[12] Backus interpreted this with 1 Corinthians 9:14: "They which preach the gospel should live of the gospel." In other words, he argued for voluntarism in church finances, rather than state support of religion. Sixth, he maintained that the "end of civil government is the *good* of the governed."[13] This, he felt, necessitated that government should guard the religious liberty of the citizenry and stop those who attempted to "invade the religious rights of others."[14] Seventh, and lastly, Backus felt that special religious privilege for a stated sect was on the wane. He related this growing idea to a sort of comming millennium (Isaiah 11:9 and Micah 4:1-4). His optimism at this point seems to border on a cessation of all selected privilege, thus resulting in a free and open state in religious concerns.

Backus stood in the historic line of the Anabaptists of Europe and the Rhode Islanders. However, there were some distinct dif-

10. Ibid., p. 436.
11. Ibid., p. 436.
12. Ibid., p. 437.
13. Ibid., p. 438.
14. Ibid., p. 438.

ferences. He and his Separatists were products of a spiritual revival whereas Williams and Clarke were not. The Rhode Island pioneers were college educated. Backus received only an elementary training. Thus, a number of differences project themselves. Backus was in basic theological agreement with his Baptist forebears but he went beyond to a personal "pietism." To Backus conversion was the answer—a very democratic answer to the Massachusetts oligarchy. They argued that ignorant fanatics needed to be kept in line by the educated clergy. Backus asserted a strong priesthood-of-the-believer position; conversion, not education, is the first and primary prerequisite for Scriptural understanding. Christian experience is the essential fount of knowledge, not education. He did not oppose education; rather, he limited it.

This, in turn, prepared the way for the Baptists to become more and more a common man's movement. It provided a simple democratic form of government for each church—one in which the simple saint could participate. It was Backus' answer to New England's clerical oligarchy. This ideal also attacked New England's static, and somewhat snobbish, class structure.

In sum, Backus provoked a movement toward an open break with the past. Williams and Clarke attempted no change of the establishment. They moved to the frontier to found a state where full religious liberty was provided. Their experiment became a model of success but it did not immediately nor noticeably alter the New England oligarchy. Backus remained, and with the zeal of his newfound faith he agitated for religious freedom within the system. One might say that Clarke and Williams provided New England with a prefiguration of what lay in the future. Backus fulfilled the prophecy. His common man's church formed a breach in the wall of the established aristocracy. He passed the Rhode Island experiment by setting in motion a force strong enough to put an end to persecution and ostracism. It was also powerful enough to disestablish a privileged church which had enjoyed a religious monopoly for nearly two centuries. It was to be the beginning of the end of a Standing Order Church.

Four
The Progress of Dissent:
To Virginia and Back Again

New England in Reverse

New England's way was not Virginia's way. New England was bent on purifying Anglicanism from afar. Virginia was satisfied with the Church of England and, therefore, sought no continuing Reformation. A previous chapter traced the earliest beginnings of the Anglican establishment in the various states, especially where Baptists were influential. The present chapter concerns itself with the dissenting Baptist tradition in Virginia. Like New England, Virginia became a center of Baptist growth and influence.

The early monopoly of the Church of England began to give way in the eighteenth century. As early as the 1660s the Quakers had attempted settlement within the colony. They were forced out due to restrictive measures on the part of the government. After England's famed Act of Toleration (1689), migration and immigration pushed at Virginia's formidable legislative laws against nonconformity. Presbyterians, Baptists and Methodists soon made deep inroads. From New England and the middle colonies came the various dissenting groups. They began to pioneer the back country, away from Virginia's tidewater plantation area where the colony's landed aristocracy controlled politics and religion. From France came the Huguenots, fleeing rising persecution following the revocation of the Edict of Nantes in 1685. All of these elements proved a threat to the Anglicans. Resistance to nonconformity grew, was challenged by the dissenters, and then gave way. The Baptist influence toward this dissent and disestablishment was one of the greatest factors.

In New England the church dominated the state. In Virginia their roles were reversed. The New England magistrates were the "nursing fathers" to the church. They were charged with enforcing both "tables of the law" and with punishing schismatics.[1] Beyond this, however, the Congregational Church was allowed a relatively free reign. The religious tax levied on the citizenry assured a sound financial base. It did not begin to give way until the late seventeenth century, and then only slowly.

In Virginia, on the other hand, the state determined the progress of the church. True, Anglicanism was fully established. It was also fully controlled. Virginia's House of Burgesses decreed what the Church of England could and could not do, to a large measure at any rate. The established clergy held sole right to perform marriages and bury the dead. A dissenter had no choice but to use their services in these matters. Then, too, the church held large parcels of plebe lands bought at public expense and given to the establishment. The clergy was supported by a stipend system. Virginia was essentially a mercantile venture and its main commodity was in smoke—tobacco was king. Clerical salaries were in the form of stipends fixed by the law in pounds of tobacco, the crop being widely used as a currency in Virginia. Thus, while Anglican ministers were state supported, they were also state regulated. Beginning in 1662 and continuing for nearly a century afterward, Virginia's General Assembly required ministers to present evidence of ordination by an English bishop. The governor

---

1. Ferm, ed. *Readings,* p. 604.

and his council were empowered with authority to silence all other persons if they attempted to preach.

Then, as now, tobacco was controversial. In Virginia's early days the issue was price, not health. Poor crops in 1755 forced a rise in prices. Payments in fixed pounds of tobacco created a special hardship on church vestries. The Virginia Assembly, hoping to relieve the problem, made debts payable at a rate of two pence a pound, much less than the going price of six cents.[2] The law affected all creditors and officers of the government, but it especially hurt the clergy.

The Anglican ministers protested by inducing the Board of Trade to have Great Britain invalidate the act of the Virginia Assembly. The British government complied. The clergy also tried to force their parishioners to pay the difference between the two pence legal rate and the six cent going rate. One pastor, a Reverend James Maury, sued for back salary since he had been paid at the new rate and with paper money. This controversy, known as the "Parson's case," came to Patrick Henry's attention in 1763.[3] On behalf of the vestry he resisted the British government's decision. He argued that the king's veto of Virginia's action amounted to tyranny. As a result the parson received a penny for damages! This whole affair created an unpopular press for the Anglican clergy and encouraged dissenters, whose numbers had now considerably grown.

The Baptists: Protest and Persecution

The Baptists were the first to enter the war for religious liberty in Virginia. Their influence and numerical strength had grown as a result of the Great Awakening. They and the Presbyterians were both deeply affected by the revival. Both groups attacked the lethargy of the Anglican establishment.

2. Stokes and Pfeffer, *Church and State*, p. 66.
3. Ibid., p. 66.

The Anglican churches were under the supervision of the vestries which, in turn, were controlled by local squires whose religious qualifications were often suspect. The clergymen were perfunctory in their preaching; and their message, of seeming unimportance, was frequently ignored. The whole church functioned as the religious arm of the aristocratic social structure of eastern Virginia's tidewater section. The Baptists and Presbyterians burst over the Blue Ridge into western Virginia and North Carolina with revival zeal, threatening to disturb the formalism of the Anglican way.

Among the Baptists were men of the caliber of Shubal Stearns and Daniel Marshall. They were New Light Baptists, in the Calvinistic tradition of Isaac Backus. Stearns, a former New England Congregationalist, arrived in 1754. These Separate Baptists, as they became known, established forty-three churches in seventeen years, their first congregation being the Sandy Creek Church of North Carolina. In 1787 the Regular and Separate Baptists had united under the framework of the Philadelphia Confession. They formed "the United Baptist churches in Virginia."[4]

With a Calvinistic theology adapted to the evangelistic techniques of the Awakening, these pioneer Baptist preachers pushed into western Virginia and North Carolina, establishing church after church. They were often without formal training and always without government sanction. They won many followers, so many in fact that alarm spread among the opposing established churches. A clash was inevitable. Between 1768 and 1776 the colony imprisoned more than forty Baptist preachers. This was relatively easy since they had no state certification. But all this persecution provided them with notorious popularity resulting in more Baptists and more dissenting congregations. By 1772 these dissenters were strong enough to begin their extended series of strongly worded memorials (a form of petitioning) to Virginia's General Assembly.

4. Vedder, *A Short History*, p. 318.

John Leland: "The Liberty I Contend for Is More Than Toleration"

Virginia became a pivotal colony in the press for complete religious liberty in America. The move toward denominational pluralism was under way in several colonies before the Revolution. The Constitutional Convention, meeting in 1787 in Philadelphia, did not go too far in the matter of religious freedom, probably because it was felt that the various colonies (now states) were already caring for this matter. In Virginia, for example, a Bill of Rights had been adopted in June of 1776, some three weeks before the Declaration of Independence. This document was drafted by George Mason, with the exception of Article Sixteen which dealt with religious freedom. The latter was the composition of Patrick Henry. This Bill of Rights exerted a considerable influence on Jefferson's Declaration on July 4, 1776.

To fully appreciate Virginia's changed posture one must go back to 1772. As before mentioned, at that time the persecuted Baptists presented the first memorial for liberty to the House of Burgesses. From then until disestablishment the conflict was intense.

Virginia provided a number of notables who strongly advocated church-state separation and religious liberty. Among them were Thomas Jefferson, James Madison, George Mason, Patrick Henry, Samuel Davies and John Leland. These men provide us with a study in contrasts. Jefferson, a lauded aristocratic planter, was opposed to the Federalists and was a deist in religion. Madison, who had once studied for the ministry at the College of New Jersey (Princeton), was an Anglican. George Mason was an Anglican. Samuel Davies was a fiery Presbyterian preacher who had influenced Henry. Henry was an Anglican layman who fought for religious liberty, with some lapses in conviction. He frequently defended dissenters in Virginia's courts, often paying their fines. Gaustad contends that his famous and fiery speech in St. John's Episcopal Church in Richmond was a cry for liberty of "both body and soul."[5]

5. Gaustad, *A Religious History,* p. 117.

Among this diverse but determined group of advocates of full religious liberty, none stands out more than the Calvinistic Baptist, John Leland (1754-1841). He was born at Grafton, Massachusetts, the son of James and Lucy (Warren) Leland. John was a descendant of Henry Leland, who came to Massachusetts from England in 1652.

His education was scanty, being limited to an elementary training in one of New England's "common schools." The chief books formulating his schooling were the Bible, John Bunyan's *Pilgrim's Progress* and Philip Doddridge's *Rise and Progress of Religion in the Soul*.[6]

Beginning as a Congregationalist, Leland embraced the much despised Baptist position. He was immersed and thereupon united with the Baptist church in Bellingham. At eighteen years of age he obeyed "a sign from God" and forsook a life of secular employment for that of the Baptist ministry. His home church granted him a preacher's license and in 1776 he left for Virginia with his new bride, Sarah Devine, whom he had married on September 30.

He settled in Orange County. In August of 1777 Leland was ordained by the Mount Poney Baptist Church without the customary "laying on of hands." This was to prove a barrier to fellowship with many of the Baptists in Virginia; so ten years later, in June of 1787, he was reordained, this time "with laying on of hands." Mr. Leland was really suited toward an itinerant ministry. In his fifteen years in Virginia he traveled extensively as an evangelist among the colony's Baptists.

In 1791 Leland removed from Virginia to Cheshire, Massachusetts, his native state. In the fifteen years in Virginia, and during the last years in Massachusetts until his death in 1841, he fought in the front ranks of the Baptists for the cause of freedom of conscience. In the same period he greatly aided the cause of Baptist church growth. In 1810 Mr. Leland related that he had baptized nearly twelve hundred people. His headstone epitaph is fitting:

6. Smith, Handy and Loetscher, *American Christianity,* Vol. 1, p. 469.

"Here lies the body of John Leland, who labored to promote piety, and vindicate the civil and religious rights of man."[7]

Leland was never a quiet fellow. Given to wit, possessed of a keen and self-educated mind, his conduct sometimes bordered on the erratic. He once baptized a woman convert whose husband threatened to murder him with a gun if he went through with the baptism. Leland dispatched a small garrison from his congregation. They detained the irate husband while he performed the ordinance.

Backus relates another interesting detail of this champion of Baptists. He became known in later years as the "mammoth priest."[8] When he settled back in Massachusetts some former friends provided him with a huge cheese to take to Virginia for presentation to his friend, President Jefferson. Leland made a four-month preaching tour out of the affair. He preached seventy-four times, drawing crowds through clever advertising of his thirteen-hundred-pound mammoth cheese![8]

Leland is remembered, however, as the greatest advocate of religious freedom which the Baptists produced following Backus. He was a member of the General Committee of the Baptists of Virginia. This organization was to these dissenters what the Warren Baptist Association's Grievance Committee was to the New England Baptists. It had been organized in 1784 to seek redress of civil and religious grievances.

In 1786 Leland, working through the committee, exercised great influence in obtaining a favorable passage of Thomas Jefferson's historic Virginia Statute of Religious Liberty. By 1777 the dissenting forces had succeeded in having the statutes repealed which had required church attendance and universal support of the established church. Not until 1779 was the Virginia Episcopal Church disestablished. But even these two advances in the cause were not sufficient, so Jefferson composed his statute. This pro-

7. Ibid., p. 470.
8. Backus, *History of New England,* p. 473.

posal provided for complete divorce of church and state.[9] Some of the leadership, such as George Washington and Patrick Henry, had argued for equal footing and state support for all Christian churches. Both of the above-mentioned men were eventually to back away from this position. Complete separation was in the wind and Virginia's leadership knew it.

Jefferson's Statute of Religious Liberty was to make an uphill fight, finally becoming Virginia's law on January 16, 1786. Jefferson was absent from the Virginia House at the time of its passage. It was sponsored by his friends Mason, Madison, Taylor, George and Nicholas. The document aroused worldwide comment. An historic precedent was set. Rhode Island had created the first state with full religious liberty. Now Virginia had entered the record as the first government to establish a full divorce between church and state, where a union had formerly existed. John Leland and his fellow Baptists were influential in its passage. Sweet quotes F. L. Hawks, an Episcopal historian, as saying, "The Baptists were the principal promoters of this work."[10]

Back Home

Leland was to figure in the cause of religious liberty with regard to the federal constitution, an item to be covered in the next chapter. Further, upon his return to Massachusetts he stood with Backus and other Baptists in the great cause of freedom in his native New England.

In 1791 he returned to accept the pastorate of the Third Baptist Church at Cheshire, Massachusetts. That same year he published his pamphlet *The Rights of Conscience Inalienable, and, Therefore, Religious Opinions Not Recognizable by Law: Or, the high-flying Churchman, stripped of his legal Robe, appears a Yaho* (New London, 1791). We will examine this document as to his thought at a later point.

9. Henry Steele Commanger, ed. *Documents of American History,* pp. 125, 126.

10. William W. Sweet, *Religion on the American Frontier, The Baptists,* 1783-1830, p. 16.

In 1806, as a leader for the Connecticut Baptists, Leland published another pamphlet of note entitled *Van Tromp.* In this one he advocated that a constitutional convention be called to adopt a new legal instrument providing full religious liberty. In twelve years' time (1818) Connecticut followed through on this suggestion.

Finally, in 1820 a constitutional convention was held in his native Massachusetts. Leland took to print once again. This time the effort was entitled *Short Essays on Government.* He proposed an amendment for the separation of church and state. In 1833 Massachusetts obliged with full disestablishment. Leland died in 1841 in his eighty-seventh year. The Baptists, and all dissenters, had lost an able spokesman.

The Rights of Conscience

What were the thought patterns of John Leland? We know of his Calvinism in theology and his Baptist convictions in church polity. He was a Calvinist but, like Backus, he did not go the route of John Gill. He felt that the use of persuasion and means were needed in preaching. Yet, he did not move to the Wesleyan pattern. He suggested that a proper proportion in preaching was "two grains of Arminianism with three of Calvinism."[11] In other words, he was a Calvinist but a product of the post-Great Awakening era. Like Backus, he not only advocated revival preaching, he actually enjoyed it. Leland had taken an active part in the second Great Awakening, a post-Revolutionary revival beginning in 1786. It had started as a Presbyterian movement and soon swept through the Congregationalists, the Baptists, the Methodists, and even some Lutherans and Episcopalians. It was a frontier awakening, especially strong in western Pennsylvania, Virginia, Kentucky and North Carolina.

Leland, like most Baptists of the period, preached a moderate Calvinism supported by a revival enthusiasm. Further, the Baptist

11. Thomas Armitage, *A History of the Baptists,* p. 788.

concept of church government was very democratic. These two features, functioning in concert, formed an appealing message to this frontier pioneering class of people. This was to prove a major factor in the Baptist "grass-roots" growth. Leland's power as a preacher was natural, robust, witty and often eccentric. What he lacked in academic polish he made up in common appeal. It was just the proper combination, divinely ordained, to meet the need of the frontier. Though lacking formal training, Leland was an astute thinker. An examination of his 1791 pamphlet, *The Rights of Conscience Inalienable,* mentioned earlier, provides the student of his thought with excellent "grist" for the mind. This had been composed upon his return to Massachusetts and was intended as an appeal to the legislature for full religious liberty.

He began by posing a question, "Are the rights of conscience alienable, or inalienable?" He defined conscience as a "censor morum" over man's conduct. Leland accepted the compact theory of government, in harmony with the political and religious theory of the Enlightenment. The big question was not whether a man surrendered some of his sovereignty upon entering this "social compact," but rather, could he surrender his conscience or, by formulating laws, bind his offspring's conscience?

To the above question Leland answered no, and asserted four arguments. First, "Every man must give account of himself to God." This was clearly a Biblical beginning. It was an obvious allusion to Romans 14:12. Next, it would be a matter of sin for a man to surrender to another man that which is reserved for God. Third, even granting a man's right to bind his own conscience, it is clearly wrong to bind his child's. Fourth, religion is a personal matter and is not the domain of civil control. He then ended the section by refuting the establishment argument that both state and religion will disappear and atheism will prevail without government control. His refutation briefly surveyed history. Christianity flowered under persecution. He took care to mention the few places where church-state separation was the prevailing practice and where both state and religion flourished. Conspicuous, of course, was Rhode Island.

The second section presents the "evils of such an establishment." These are five in number. First, fallible man makes his own test of what is orthodox. If one way is approved it could well be the wrong way. Second, such an establishment weakens the body politic, for it leads those in a minority toward mutiny or migration. Third, the established church itself will become a tool of the state. Some will conclude that "Bible religion" is naught but a "trick of the state." Fourth, since no two governments establish quite the same official church, then surely both cannot be right and both may be wrong. Finally, an established church prevents the best of men from seeking civil office. "Good men cannot believe what they cannot believe." If the state requires an oath of office in harmony with the established church's doctrine, then a "villain" will commit perjury and a qualified man will simply not offer himself unless he can agree with the religious oath.

Leland then listed the causes of state establishment of religion. There are five. First, "the love of importance is a general evil." Next, many are anxious to promote a particular sect. Here he presented Constantine by way of example. Third, there is the motive of producing "uniformity in religion." On this point Leland argued that the truth must stand for its own defense. Fourth was the "common objection" that religion must be established by the state since the "ignorant part of the community" cannot fend for themselves in an effort to discover the true way. Here he clearly struck at the New England and Virginia religious aristocracy. Fifth, and finally, "clerical influence" has established religion in the state.

But what prompted the Massachusetts magistrates that they should be "nursing fathers" to the church? Clearly it is the clergy's flattery. (It was common for the New England clergy to preach election-day sermons, urging out the vote. It also stimulated the godly to run for office. A point not out of order, except the clergy had in mind those who would further the cause of established religion.) What prompted the clergy to flatter the civil leadership? Leland proposed three answers in short, terse statements. First, "ignorance"—that is, they could not refute error by argument.

Second, "indolence"—the clergy was too lazy to bother refuting error. Third, "money"—the New England cleric knew where his salary originated. It was not from freewill giving, but from the state taxation to support the Standing Order ministers.[12]

What Leland proposed, by way of substitute for the tyranny of established religion, is disclosed in his *Short Essays on Government* (1820). "The liberty I contend for is more than toleration." To Leland a degree of toleration already existed, in some small measure at least. It was a toleration grudgingly granted by a supposed superior or preeminent group to an obviously lower and minority cast. Leland had only contempt for such condescending aristocratic notions. To be free in religion means to be totally at liberty to espouse or deny any view. Care need only be taken to prevent encroachment on the rights of others. All should be "equally free, Jews, Turks, Pagans, and Christians." The plagues of society were "Test Oaths and Established Creeds." To Leland, creed and oath were the domain of a church, not the state.[13]

In all of this Leland proved himself, in the first place, a student of Scripture. His argument began with the Pauline concept in the Book of Romans. However, he ranged to other intellectual pastures. His concept of church and state separation was, in some measure, in the tradition of that leader of the English Enlightment, John Locke, although he does not quote him. Locke's *Second Treatise of Government* (1690) was his major contribution in the realm of political theory. Locke advocated a large degree of religious toleration and a civil society in which man is bound together by means of a "contract."

It is far more likely that Leland had been influenced to embrace Lockean ideas by his good friend, Thomas Jefferson. Jefferson himself was a zealous reader of the English theorist. Many of his ideas regarding politics and religion found their source in the man. The compact theory of government, espoused by Leland, was first

12. All above quotations from *The Rights of Conscience Inalienable* are from *The Writings of John Leland,* ed. by L. F. Greene, pp. 179-199.

13. Stokes and Pfeffer, *Church and State.,* p. 63.

the child of Locke, then adapted to American soil by the anti-Federalist Jefferson.

Both Locke and Jefferson entertained deistic ideas—God exists but is unknowable. When Jefferson became President he began a series of letters in correspondence with Dr. Joseph Priestly of England and Dr. Benjamin Rush, physician, philosopher and a member of the Federal Constitutional Convention along with Jefferson, Madison and Franklin. Out of this developed Jefferson's infamous Bible project. He reduced the Bible to 25,000 words, composed of the life and moral teachings of Jesus. He never intended to publish this undertaking. In fact, it was not printed for distribution until 1904. His "Bible" ended with Christ in the tomb, thus forfeiting the Christian doctrine of resurrection.

Jefferson's pronounced deism is significant to our purpose in that, first of all, he was a good friend and fellow laborer of John Leland, the Baptist dissenter. Leland openly advocated support of Jefferson's Democratic-Republican party. He felt it the only way to break the grip of the New England Congregationalist-Federalist movement on Connecticut politics. He urged this support in spite of the many deists in Jeffersonian ranks. However, outside of the political arena, Leland fought deism with a passion. To him, this double stance was not inconsistent. So long as Jefferson openly advocated complete church-state separation, Leland would side with him. To agree with his theology was another matter. It was the echo of Roger Williams versus George Fox.

There were many differences between the Baptists and the deists. Backus and Leland stood in the Pietistic tradition. They were the product of a Biblical revival and conversion to Christ. Jefferson and his deistic friends were rationalists and naturalists. The source of authority for deism was pure reason and scientific inquiry. For the Baptists it was the Bible. Deism spoke of a nebulous "Creator." The Baptists spoke of a personal God Who has revealed Himself not simply in creation but also in revelation. It may seem strange to us, but on religious freedom they stood as one. On the content of religion they were as enemies. The controversy certainly made "strange bedfellows."

A final item in the long and lively career of this indomitable Baptist deserves notice. In 1811 Leland was elected to the Massachusetts House of Representatives, running on the Jefferson party's ticket. One must remember at this juncture of history that in early New England even the members of the Standing Order clergy were forbidden this privilege. Magistrates were always to be laymen. Indeed, the times were changing! Leland anticipated no conflict of interest. He served as a citizen, not as a clergyman.

Five
One Wall Demolished:
A Second Erected

Disestablishment in the States

A cherished way dies hard, even a severely challenged one. A state with an established church was a by-product of the European background of early America. Until Rhode Island no government in history had ever attempted such a radical innovation as complete church-state separation. What is today an accepted fact of American life and practice was in colonial America a way so novel and so threatening as to evoke the very deepest of emotions and convictions, whether favorable or adamantly opposed.

Some authorities have suggested that, in a very real sense, Martin Luther was the original founder of America. It is quite true that the North American settlers of the thirteen colonies were, as previously noted, bent on a religious quest to some degree. The majority were of Protestant background, Maryland being a notable exception. Yet, even Luther, for all his reforming patterns, offered no break with the state. His rupture was with Rome. Even that, at the first, was an unintentional break. Luther offered a national church to displace the former so-called "universal" church of Rome. A rising nationalism was on his side, but a complete severance between the state and the church was never his intention.

One can better understand Luther's reaction to Anabaptism when care is taken to note his desire to maintain, to a large degree, a monolithic church structure on German soil. The Anabaptist concept was radical, too radical for either Luther or his time. Thus, their idea of a believer's church, with a separate and secular state existing outside it, was more than the period could tolerate. The only evident recourse toward sixteenth century Anabaptism was precisely what occurred, namely violent persecution of the hapless forerunners of the modern Baptists.

To turn to Calvin or Knox or any of the other main reformers in an effort to discover sympathy for church-state separation is entirely futile. None ever existed. Puritanism, even the most radical kind such as Plymouth Separatism, was more akin to Calvinism in its view of the church and state than toward European Anabaptism. The Massachusetts oligarchy never had a Rhode Island in mind. Their ideal formulation was Calvin's Geneva. Let the church and the state function in harmony and allow the godly to rule both.

But the tide of history in America pushed against this concept of church-state union until it tottered and fell. It did not arrive in a single moment or with a single event. Rather, one section of the wall fell and then another.

To begin with, disestablishment was not needed in Rhode Island. As before related, this historic Baptist colony set a precedent to be envied and copied by those to follow. Penn's Pennsylvania likewise provided a separation between state and church. Liberty was not of the same degree as that which existed in Rhode Island. In the latter, one could accept or deny any religious tenet and not forfeit his civil rights. In Pennsylvania one had to believe in one God in order to be a citizen. Further, he had to espouse a belief in Christ in order to hold office. Beyond this, no religious restriction was placed upon the citizenry. Maryland was the only other early attempt at religious liberty. Lord Baltimore's experiment in behalf of his English Roman Catholics was doomed to failure within a few years of the famed Toleration Act of 1649. The Maryland venture, unlike Rhode Island, seems to have had both religious and economic reasons for its offer of toleration. Religious liberty was limited to Roman Catholics, Anglicans and most Protestants. Since one had to profess belief in Christ, it was no haven for the Jews, Unitarians or atheists.

The heroes of full religious liberty in Virginia—including the Baptist, John Leland—finally won their victory. The last vestige of establishment was the vacant plebe land owned by the Episcopal Church. This issue was settled in 1802 when the Virginia Assembly ordered a system for returning this property to private ownership with payments for the sales going to worthy non-religious purposes.[1] Virginia had accomplished full religious liberty and church-state separation. This action proved a forerunner for the other fledgling states.

The struggle in Massachusetts was both long and arduous. It was the stronghold of the Congregational-Federalist system. Williams and Clarke provided the first breach in the wall, although it was hastily repaired. Backus and Leland fought valiantly, and the latter saw the wall maintaining Congregationalism finally collapse.

The first move toward this final goal was John Adams' Declaration of Rights, which formed a part of the state constitution of 1780.[2] It had one limitation. The much-hated Article Three, the object of Backus' most severe attacks, was contained in this document. It provided for state support of religion, although it allowed for a taxpayer's payment to be applied to a sect or denomination named by him, with the understanding that this be a Protestant enterprise.

By 1820 the opportunity came for a constitutional convention. An amendment to lift the restrictions of Article Three was proposed. Leland's *Short Essay on Government* set forth this amendment concept. Unfortunately, the voters defeated this proposal

---

1. Stokes and Pfeffer, *Church and State*, p. 71.
2. Ibid., p. 77.

for religious liberty by a margin of nine thousand votes.[3] Undaunted, the Baptists continued to press for total separation.

The last blow against this supposed impregnable wall in Massachusetts came in 1833. The electorate disestablished Congregationalism and provided that henceforth all religious groups were to be self-governing and self-supporting. The ratio favoring this move was ten to one.[4] Standing in opposition to those who espoused a full divorce between church and state were many venerable Congregational clergy, but it was Connecticut which offered the most able leadership for the status quo.

Connecticut was the child of Massachusetts in both church and state. Nowhere was Congregationalism more firmly in control. The Standing Order clergy held sway for many years after the War of Independence, controlling the governor's side of the legislature. Their leadership was awesome: Timothy Dwight (1752-1817), a descendant of Jonathan Edwards and a leader of the Second Awakening; Lyman Beecher (1775-1863), a student of Dwight's at Yale; and Nathaniel Taylor (1786-1858), a Yale professor. Of the three, Taylor later became the outstanding theorist of the modified Calvinistic school, sometimes referred to as the "New England Theology." This movement was the intellectual offspring of Edwards, plus being the champion of the Standing Order.

The Connecticut established clergy, almost to a man, stood behind Dwight in opposition to Jefferson's election in 1800. Of all the dissenters, the most vocal were the Baptists. From 1802 to 1818 they petitioned the legislature every year in behalf of total separation and religious freedom. Backus died in 1806 but his mantle of leadership fell on the able Leland. The latter rallied the Baptists and other dissenters behind the much despised Democratic-Republican party. Deism, an European heresy, had spread among the Congregationalists. It weakened the system, especially

3. Ibid., p. 77.
4. Ibid., p. 77.

by alluring leadership away from the established church and the Federalist party.

Congregationalists enjoyed special favor until 1818. In that year a new constitution provided full freedom in religion, but the wording implied that only Christianity was recognized.[5] Strangely, Beecher, who fought the outcome to the bitter end, stated his candid opinion that it was a healthy decision for both state and church.[6]

New Hampshire had adopted a constitution in 1783. On the question of religion it followed the Massachusetts model, with the inclusion of a provision quite similar to the much-dreaded Article Three. By 1852 the restriction barring non-Protestants from holding office was dropped. The present New Hampshire constitution provides a large degree of religious liberty and full separation; but as late as 1964 its Bill of Rights still had a section implying favor to Protestantism, with another speaking of "Christians," which could be construed to bar Jews from some civil privilege. This document even has a section allowing for some civil support of "public Protestant teachers."[7] While these limitations exist on paper they are not enforced.

The first state admitted to the Union, beyond the thirteen, was Vermont (1791). Its constitution (1777) was patterned after that of Pennsylvania (1776) and allowed great religious liberty except that it forbade non-Protestants from holding civil office. By 1793 it had provided amendments to the constitution establishing full freedom and no religious test for officeholding.

Moving to New York, one discovers that as late as 1784 the Episcopal Church was established in four counties near New York City. In 1777 the constitutional convention provided a phrase in its legislative document somewhat related to Virginia's Bill of Rights (1776). John Jay offered an amendment to exclude the Roman Catholics from nearly all civil liberty unless they swore an

5. Ibid. p. 75.

6. Gaustad, *A Religious History*, p. 132.

7. Stokes and Pfeffer, *Church and State*, p. 78.

oath of anti-papal sentiments.[8] The convention softened Jay's proposal considerably but did not lift a test oath restriction against Catholics. In 1784 the Episcopal church was finally disestablished and in 1806 the test oath was abolished.

North and South Carolina became separate colonies in 1712. The Anglicans were in the majority in the early days. Quite naturally, establishment was the desire. In 1778 South Carolina formulated its constitution. It established "the Christian Protestant Religion."[9] To be a citizen one had to "acknowledge" one God and accept a concept of a "future state" with "reward" and "punishment."

Further, any group of Protestants desiring to form a religious body in South Carolina had to be incorporated, and the incorporation had to pass five tests. First, like the individual, it had to acknowledge "one eternal God" and a "future state," including the concept of "rewards" and "punishments." Second, the religious body had to agree that God was to be "publicly" worshiped. Third, they had to submit to a belief in the exclusiveness of Christianity as the "true religion." Fourth, they had to maintain a belief in the inspiration and authority of both testaments of the Bible. This effectively eliminated Jews, atheists and agnostics. Finally, the religious corporation had to agree that every citizen had a duty to "bear witness to the truth." To become a legally recognized religious body, fifteen or more men of legal age had to agree to the above tenets and seek incorporation under South Carolina law as a "Christian Protestant Church." They then became a part of the state religious establishment. The document provided that the "Church of England" was already a recognized religious body.[10]

In 1790 South Carolina replaced this constitution with a new one which granted complete religious liberty, with one exception—no clergyman could hold civil office.

The Baptist influence in South Carolina's move to disestablish-

8. Ibid., p. 73.
9. Ibid., p. 78.
10. Ibid., p. 79.

ment was not significant. Their movement was small and scattered until the latter part of the eighteenth century. Before 1751 only five Baptist churches existed in this colony. Between that date and 1780 thirty Baptist churches were established. Thus, while they must have rejoiced at the door of liberty now opened, the Baptist role in the struggle was not as pronounced as elsewhere.

In North Carolina the story was different. Baptists from the north had begun a work as early as 1727. The first churches were General Baptists of Arminian persuasion. By 1754 the Calvinistic Separate Baptists, with Stearns and Marshall as the important leaders, had arrived in Virginia and North Carolina. In 1760 the Separate Baptists of the two colonies had formed the Sandy Creek Association. In a ten-year period (1760-1770) this fellowship expanded at a pace seldom equaled in Baptist history.[11]

With such growth and members the Baptists were in position to carry the fight for religious liberty to the highest authorities. In 1711 the North Carolina legislature had allowed Protestant dissenters a degree of freedom, in keeping with England's Act of Toleration (1689). However, between 1730 and 1773 dissenters were prevented from holding virtually all offices in the colony and many private positions of influence as well. When the colony declared its independence from Great Britain (1776), dissenters were allowed to perform marriages. No one was imprisoned, as had been the case in Virginia; but dissenters were compelled to support the established Anglican Church by taxation, plus suffer the restrictions of the Schism and Marriage Acts.

In 1773 the Vestry Act had run its legal course and was not renewed. This effectively disestablished the state church. The new constitution of 1776 provided a Bill of Rights. The Scotch-Irish Presbyterians were first in influencing this decisive legislation, followed by the Baptists. It was limited in that non-Protestants could not hold civil office and clergymen could not function in the legislature. In 1835 the latter restriction was lifted and political

11. Sweet, History of *Religion on the American Frontier,* p. 7.

offices were opened "to all Christians."[12] In 1868 this restriction, which prevented Jews from holding office, was removed; the only remaining requirement was a belief in God.

Delaware never suffered from an established church. William Penn's influence was responsible in this matter. Its 1776 constitution prevented the recognition of any state religion. However, clergymen and those denying the Trinity were disqualified from public office. This religious test was outlawed in 1792.

By 1776 Pennsylvania had adopted a constitution. It included a statement providing religious liberty, though, in fact, liberty was already practiced. However, a religious test for members of the legislature was imposed which required belief in "one God" and assent to the inspiration of both testaments of the Bible.[13] This was altered in 1790, but a restriction excluding atheists or agnostics from public office was still in effect as late as 1964 though not enforced.

Georgia adopted a constitution in 1777 which provided a large measure of liberty but required that a taxpayer pay for his own church support by a religious tax. In 1798 this requirement was dropped.

Maryland disestablished the Anglican Church in 1776 with its adoption of a constitution. It excluded non-Christians from public office until 1826.

New Jersey had allowed Quaker settlements in the early days. Therefore, a more open spirit of toleration was evident from the first. Along with many others, it declared independence from Great Britain and drew up a constitution in 1776 which provided religious toleration for all and disallowed any establishment. However, only Protestants were eligible for civil office. This remained unchanged until 1874.

Thus, we have traced the effort that led to disestablishment in the first thirteen states plus Vermont from start to finish. The Baptist influence in this state by state struggle was greatest in

12. Stokes and Pfeffer, *Church and State,* p. 92.
13. Ibid., p. 80.

Massachusetts, Connecticut, Virginia and North Carolina. These were the Baptist strongholds where the movement had established large beachheads among the more common classes of people. Of the total individual state efforts only two really provided what could be construed as full liberty. Rhode Island offered it from the beginning and Virginia conceded to it by 1802 when the church-owned plebe lands were sold. In all the other twelve states some remaining vestige of establishment lingered on. In most cases it was a matter of public law, still standing but no longer enforced. It can safely and accurately be asserted that when Massachusetts moved to disestablish the Congregational Church in 1833 the battle had finally been won. America stood on the edge of a political experiment quite unlike anything previously experienced in history. Among the other religious forces, the Baptists had played their essential role.

One Article and One Amendment

With Cornwallis' surrender to Washington at Yorktown on October 19, 1781, the colonies had nearly fulfilled the vision of independence. Now the problem was, independence to do what? The answer lay in the years between 1776 and 1790. First came the agony of the Articles of Confederation, the early attempt at formulating a new government and nation. By May of 1787 the first constitutional convention convened in Philadelphia. Not until May 29, 1790, would the new document be fully ratified by all thirteen colonies. Significantly, the last outpost of negative reaction was Rhode Island, that Baptist bastion of the "otherwise minded." They actually voted for ratification after the constitution was in force. Their vote on the matter is of interest. Thirty-four delegates were favorable and thirty-two opposed!

Jefferson's Declaration of Independence contained several references to the Person of God. He used deistic language such as the "Creator" and "nature's God." Ten years later the federal constitution would contain no reference to God, except as to the date of its signing, and only two references to religion. Both of these were by way of prohibition. This apparent absence of reference to God in America's major legislative instrument created heated debate. Timothy Dwight of Yale College criticized this omission as the work of Jefferson.[14]

The real point of interest lies in Article Six and Amendment One of the Bill of Rights. The former states as to religion, "But no religious test shall ever be required as a qualification to any office or public trust under the United States." The latter declares, "Congress shall make no law respecting an establishment of religion, or prohibiting the free exercise thereof." Article Six, therefore, prohibits the matter of a religious test oath required on the part of civil officeholders. This provision precludes the government becoming a bondslave to a particular church. The First Amendment, on the other hand, eliminates the establishment of a preferred sect, thus preventing religion, on the whole, from being hindered by government decree. The source of these two provisions is of interest.

First of all one must remember that church-state separation was, at the time, being fought out at the state level. Apparently, the Founding Fathers felt these two statements represented the best pronouncement in view of the various state provisions for religious liberty.

Article Six was part of the original document and hence was drafted in 1787. At that time, as before noted, all New England except Rhode Island still had Congregationalism established. The Church of England had just been disestablished in Virginia, North Carolina and Georgia. South Carolina and Maryland yet retained a state Episcopal Church. Rhode Island, Pennsylvania and Delaware did not have an established church. New Jersey and New York had some small remnants of establishment. Concerning Baptist influence on Article Six, Isaac Backus stood at the front. He traveled to Philadelphia representing the Warren Baptist Association. He strongly urged the delegates to embrace a course of full

14. Ibid., p. 90.

liberty of conscience and prohibition of a tax to support a state church.

Backus and Leland strongly supported the federal constitution, provided it fully guaranteed complete church-state separation and absolute religious liberty. Both men found support for the idea of a central government in the tradition of the Enlightenment. Several of the Founding Fathers were "enlightened." Among them were Jefferson, Franklin, Adams, Hamilton and Paine. John Locke was the titular English head of this movement, which enshrined reason as man's best hope. In harmony with this, the Enlightenment embraced the compact theory of government in which a man gave up some measure of independence for the common good. To these naturalists this social contract was based upon man's inherent rights. Neither Backus nor Leland agreed with this. Jefferson argued for man's "inalienable rights." To him this was the basis of a central government. It must be strong enough to protect his freedom but not so powerful as to rob him of it. Leland and Backus asserted that government is necessary since man is a sinner. Government is the expression of total depravity. Man lost his original freedom by violating "the rules of government."[15]

While neither Backus nor Leland were deeply read in the Enlightenment literature of the period, they were willing to accept the compact or social contract idea of government. But both men insisted on limiting the theory. Leland, for example, embraced the social contract but declared that this in no way could bind a man's conscience.[16] Backus agreed with him and both men argued the point from Scripture. In simple terms they were Biblicists and Baptists. The Bible said the conscience could not be bound by men but only by God or the devil. The Baptist concept of individual soul liberty concurred.

Actually, the presentation of Article Six was the work of Charles Pickney, an Anglican from South Carolina. His motives

15. Backus, *Isaac Backus on Church, State and Calvinism,* ed. by Wm. G. McLoughlin, p. 42.
16. Smith, Handy and Loetscher, *American Christianity,* Vol 1, p. 470.

were clear. He desired to free all government offices from a religious test oath. In the second place, the words preceding the particular section on religion specify that all persons holding office "shall be bound by oath or affirmation." The last two words Pickney included to allow Quakers to hold office since their convictions prevented oath-taking. On August 30, 1787, Article Six was passed, thus erecting one section of the church-state wall of separation. Aside from the presidential elections of 1928 and 1960 there has been little debate regarding the interpretation of Article Six.

The same cannot be said for the First Amendment. It has been a storm center of controversy almost from inception. On May 4, 1789, Madison announced to the House of Representatives assembled in New York that he intended to present the subject of constitutional amendments. What he had in mind was a Bill of Rights to further insure personal liberties. On June 8, Madison urged the adoption of these historic ten amendments. They were ratified by the several states in 1791. For our discussion, the First Amendment is of vital importance.

In 1788 John Leland was still heading the Baptist drive for full religious liberty in Virginia. In that same year he wrote a letter to Washington on behalf of the General Committee of the Baptists in Virginia. He began by relating the Baptist apprehension growing out of persecution. On one hand they feared the lack of federal union would result in anarchy. Yet, said Leland, the desire for national unity may hide "religious oppression" if one group should "predominate over the rest." He expressed a feeling, however, that the plan must be good even if "religious liberty is rather insecure in the Constitution." This, he felt, was due to Washington's willingness to preside.[17]

In 1788 Leland had been selected by the Baptists of Orange County to attend the Virginia convention with the express purpose of opposing Virginia's ratification of the federal instrument. As noted in his letter to Washington, he feared the constitution's

17. Gaustad, *A Religious History*, p. 119.

lack of explicit religious freedom. Madison led those favoring ratification. When the two met for debate, Madison won Leland to his side. Leland then proceeded to campaign for his former rival who was later elected. Leland's efforts resulted in Madison's presentation of the historic Bill of Rights, with the First Amendment guaranteeing full religious liberty. The second and final part of the wall separating church and state at the federal level had been erected.

Six
The Legacy of Dissent

When the colonies declared their independence in 1776, they set sail in largely uncharted waters. True, others had tried the path of sovereignty before, but the colonies and Great Britain were really not natural enemies. Indeed, one had sprung from the other. They held a common lineage in terms of government, laws, freedoms and religion. But the colonists were bent on going beyond—beyond king and parliament, beyond vestments and archbishops.

The Congregational way in New England and the Anglican way elsewhere were but steps toward the goal of absolute separation of church and state. Those who maintained that the establishment should remain did not think in terms of steps. In their thinking the goal was achieved. But an idea, once begun, can seldom be stopped until it has spent itself or arrived at its goal. Church-state separation, though never intended by Massachusetts and Virginia, was really a latent idea within their colonial adventure. They desired to preserve the best of the past with the novelty of the present. There was to be no rupture between the two administrations of Christ upon earth but only careful control of both. However, dissent fosters dissent. The colonial dissenters were simply saying to the New England oligarchy (formerly dissenters themselves), "Let's be on with it and see where we come out."

Where America "came out" is the trait that makes the greatness of our nation—a quality totally unique in its religious and civil heritage. To this day our European counterparts still have not achieved what America possesses in this matter.

The Legacy Is Threefold

Disestablishment at both state and national levels provided the United States with the first legacy of dissent. Church-state separation has become a fact of life for every American. Volumes have been written on this subject. Leagues have been formed to foster it. Congress and courts have defended, interpreted and maintained it. It was, however, the colonial dissenters who provided it. What is so commonly accepted by us today must have appeared a thing of monstrous proportion to those who objected in the heated debate of the past. After all, it had never really been successfully attempted.

We are indebted to those worthy and dogmatic dissenters of the past, whatever their sect. This work has attempted to emphasize only the Baptist contribution. On the surface that may appear narrow. Our only justification can be found in the fact that while many came to advocate the dissenter's way, the Baptists were first. Rhode Island will ever stand in world history as the first successful government providing complete church-state separation with "full libertie in religious concernments." In fact, after years of persecution, frustration, objecting, petitioning and formulating, Rhode Island's way has become the American way.

So strong has the conviction been molded that it has endured for over three hundred years. What is even more amazing is the success in continuing to transplant the idea. America is the melting pot of the world. With every wave of immigration there came the foreigner, often with the old opinion of the former way. Each time he must be instructed in the American way of the separation of church and state. The same can be said, to lesser degree, of each native generation. They, too, must be instructed. Though often tested, the wall between the church and the state remains today. The reason is simple—the Baptists and the other dissenters of the past have extended their thought and influence from generation to generation. When someone attempts to breach that wall, a modern Roger Williams or Isaac Backus is there to remortar the weak spot.

But the legacy of dissent goes far beyond the separation of church and state. Opposers of this unique way feared the death of Christian principles. It was an understandable fear. From their point of view they argued that if proper morals and theology are not maintained through coercion they will falter and then fail. But it did not happen. The Baptists have always been separatist in position. The government is one arm of God. The church is another. The two are to remain separate. Freedom must reign. Not all will be converted. Baptists, unlike others, have never historically held that the world can be Christianized. Quite the contrary, the business of the church is to "take out of them a people for his name" (Acts 15:14). Therefore, the church and the world are never synonymous nor are they even on the same track. Only those advocating a believer's church carry this principle to its conclusion.

By divorcing the state from the church the door was opened, not shut. It provided two other legacies of dissent. The first was religious pluralism. Simply put, the American way allows every sect to flourish and prosper or to atrophy and die. Whether the first or the second occurred was not determined by civil support or edict but by open competition in the market of humanity. This has fostered an innovation and enthusiasm not duplicated anywhere in the world. This has produced an American missionary force that is not even remotely equaled by any other on earth. The Baptist concept—"a full libertie in religious concernments," as John Clarke put it—has provided the greatest impetus for missions and church planting.

Church-state separation led to religious pluralism and pluralism led to religious voluntarism. Each, in turn, was the child of the preceding. Voluntarism has many facets. After disestablishment all churches had to obtain members through their own efforts. This became an incentive to evangelize. True, the Baptists realized that heresy could spread. To them it frequently spread under establishment anyway. Under separation, growth became dependent upon obedience to God's command to evangelize, plus His evident blessing upon such endeavors. It is no secret that the Baptists have been blessed as much or more than others under this system. Persecution made them stand and endure. Freedom allowed them to flourish.

Beyond the question of growth in numbers, voluntarism has two other aspects. First, the question of support. The Baptist way has always been easily suited to American pluralism and voluntarism. Freewill giving was their answer. Backus fought harder to erase state support of the Standing Order clergy than for any other single issue. Coercion for religious support was the nemesis of the early Baptists. Once freed from taxation to support the established church, the Baptists could channel their voluntary giving to their own enterprises.

One further area has been aided by voluntarism. This is the area of missions and the ministry. It is true men did volunteer for the ministry within the established church, but the coming of separation and voluntarism freed the ordinary man for service. Formerly, the established way was to select the clergy from the better families and send them for preparation to Harvard or Yale or, in the case of the Anglicans, to England. This system perpetuated a clerical aristocracy. Baptists appealed, in large measure, to the common man. This was especially true during and after the Great Awakening. This revival prompted a more democratic spirit. The Baptists especially benefited in this. The first prerequisite for service was conversion. The second was a divine call. Education was third and was frequently forgotten. Consequently, this prerequisite involved an element of risk and sometimes created confusion or mindless passion. The Baptists realized that education did have some value, second to Christian experience, of course. As early as 1764 they established the College of Rhode Island (Brown University) where godly youth could seek preparation for the ministry. The Rhode Islanders were helped by the Philadelphia Association in this faith venture.

Out of Retrospect: Prospect

Why tell the story of Williams, Clarke, Backus, Leland and their kind? Not simply for the novelty of history but rather as an incentive to carry on where they left off. Certainly, others did carry on the legacy, right down to the present. Each of these four Baptist pioneers was a planter of churches. Their ideals survived because Baptists survived. Even Williams, who forsook them within six months, had fathered one church. The others founded many. In spite of the heavy burden created by the battle for religious liberty, they fostered the growth of Christian churches. Twentieth-century Baptists would do well to emulate them. The strength of America lies not so much in mere documents, nor in Washington, as it does in the building of strong, sound and Bible-oriented churches.

Bibliography

Those volumes listed with the asterisk (*) are quoted in the text with permission of the publishers.

Books Containing Primary Source Material

Backus, Isaac. *A History of New England with Particular Reference to the Denomination of Christians Called Baptists.* 2nd. ed. Edited by David Weston. 2 Vols. Newton, Mass.: Backus Historical Society, 1871.

*Backus, Isaac. *Isaac Backus on Church, State and Calvinism: Pamphlets, 1754-1789.* Edited by William G. McLoughlin. Cambridge, Mass.: Harvard Universtiy Press, 1968.

Bartlett, J. R. *Records of the Colony of Rhode Island.* Providence, R.I.: Crawford, Green and Brother, 1856.

Bradford, William. *Bradford's History of the Plymouth Settlement, 1608-1650.* Rendered into Modern English by Harold Paget. New York: E. P. Dutton & Co., 1909.

Callender, John. *An Historical Discourse, on the Civil and Religious Affairs of the Colony of Rhode Island.* Edited by Romeo Elton. Providence, R. I.: Knowles, Vost & Company, 1838.

Clarke, John. *Ill News from New England: or a Narrative of New-England Persecution. Wherein Is Declared That While Old England Is Becoming New, New-England Is Become Old.* London: Printed by Henry Hills living in Fleet-Yard next door to the Rose and Crown, 1652.

Commanger, Henry Steele. ed. *Documents of American History.* (9th. ed.). Englewood Cliffs, N.J.: Prentice-Hall, Inc., 1973.

Cousins, Norman. *In God We Trust.* New York: Harper & Brothers, 1958. (Writings of the Founding Fathers regarding religion, with commentary.)

*Ferm, Robert L., ed. *Readings in the History of Christian Thought.* New York: Holt, Rinehart and Winston, Inc., 1964.

Green, Albert G. *Collections of the Rhode Island Historical Society.* Providence, R.I., Knowles, Vost and Co., 1838.

Johnson, Edward. *Johnson's Wonder-Working Providence, 1628-1651.* Edited by J. Franklin Jameson. New York: Charles Scribner's Sons, 1910.

King, Henry Melville. *A Summer Visit of Three Rhode Islanders to the Massachusetts Bay in 1651.* Providence, R.I.: Preston and Rounds, 1896.

Leland, John. *The Writings of John Leland.* Edited by L. F. Greene. New York: Reprinted by Arno Press, Inc., 1969.

*MacDonald, William, ed. *Documentary Source Book of American History, 1606-1913.* New and Enlarged Edition. New York: The MacMillan Co., 1925.

Mather, Cotton. *Magnalia Christi Americana or, The Ecclesiastical History of New England from Its First Planting in the Year 1620, unto the Year of our Lord 1698 in Seven Books.* Edited by Rev. Thomas Robbins. 2 Vols. New York: Reprinted by Russell & Russell, 1967.

Polishook, Irwin H. *Roger Williams, John Cotton and Religious Freedom.* Englewood Cliffs, N.J.: Prentice-Hall, Inc., 1967. (Quotes from the controversy between the two men, plus commentary.)

*Schaff, Philip. *The Creeds of Christendom, with a History and Critical Notes in Three Volumes.* Vol. III. 4th ed. New York: Harper & Brothers, 1919.

*Smith, Hilrie Shelton; Handy, Robert T.; and Loetscher, Lefferts. *American Christianity.* 2 Vols. New York: Charles Scribner's Sons, 1960-63. (Standard source of primary source materials relating to American religion.)

*Stokes, Anson Phelps and Pfeffer, Leo. *Church and State in the United States.* (Revised.) New York: Harper & Row, Publishers,

1964. (The standard in the field of church and state in a one volume revision with many primary quotes.)

*Sweet, William W. *Religion on the American Frontier: The Baptists–1783-1830.* (A Collection of Source Material.) New York: Henry Holt & Co., 1931.

Williams, Roger. *The Complete Writings of Roger Williams.* Vols. I-VIII. New York: Russell & Russell, 1963.

Winthrop, John, Esq. *The History of New England from 1630-1649.* Edited by James Savage. 2 Vols. Boston: Little, Brown and Company, 1853.

Secondary Sources

Armitage, Thomas. *A History of the Baptists (to the year 1886).* New York: Brian Taylor & Co., 1887.

Brockunier, Samuel Hugh. *The Irrepressible Democrat, Roger, Williams.* New York: The Ronald Press Co., 1940.

*Cairns, Earle E. *Christianity in the United States.* Chicago: Moody Press, 1964.

De Blois, Austen Kennedy. *Fighters for Freedom, Heroes of the Baptist Challenge.* Philadelphia: The Judson Press, 1929.

Fiske, John. *The Beginnings of New England, or the Puritan Theocracy in Its Relations to Civil and Religious Liberty.* Boston: Houghton Mifflin Company, 1930.

*Gaustad, Edwin Scott. *A Religious History of America.* New York: Harper & Row Publishers, 1966. (Many fine quotes from sources.)

Littell, Franklin Hamlin. *From State Church to Pluralism: A Protestant Interpretation in American History.* Garden City, N.Y.: Doubleday and Company, Inc. 1962.

McLoughlin, William G. *Isaac Backus and the American Pietistic Tradition.* Boston: Little, Brown & Co., 1967.

Mecklin, John M. *The Story of American Dissent.* New York: Harcourt, Brace and Co., 1934.

Miller, Perry. *Orthodoxy in Massachusetts; 1635-1650, a Genetic Study.* Cambridge, Mass.: Harvard University Press, 1933.

_____. *Roger Williams, His Contributions to the American Tradition.* Indianapolis: The Bobbs Merrill Co., Inc., 1953.

_____. *The New England Mind from Colony to Province.* Cambridge, Mass.: The Harvard University Press, 1953.

_____. *The New England Mind: The Seventeenth Century.* New York: The Macmillan Co., 1939.

Morgan, Edmund S. *Roger Williams: The Church and the State.* New York: Harcourt, Brace & World, Inc., 1967.

Nelson, Wilbur. *The Hero of Aquidneck, A Life of Dr. John Clarke.* New York: Fleming H. Revell, 1938.

Newman, Albert Henry. *A History of the Baptist Churches in the United States.* 6th. ed. Revised and Enlarged. New York: Charles Scribner's Sons, 1915.

Olmstead, Clifton E. *History of Religion in the United States.* Englewood Ciffs, N.J.: Prentice-Hall, Inc., 1960.

*Sweet, William W. *The Story of Religion in America.* New York: Harper Brothers, Publishers, 1950.

Trinterud, Leonard J. *The Forming of an American Tradition, A Reexamination of Colonial Presbyterianism.* Philadelphia: The Westminster Press, 1949.

*Turner, Frederick Jackson. *The Frontier in American History.* New York: Henry Holt & Co., 1920.

*Vedder, Henry C. *A Short History of the Baptists.* New and Illustrated Edition. Philadelphia: The American Baptist Publication Society, 1954.

Winslow, Ola Elizabeth. *Master Roger Williams, A Biography.* New York: The Macmillan Co., 1957. (One of the best on Williams.)

Atlas

Gaustad, Edwin Scott. *Historical Atlas of Religion in America.* New York: Harper & Row, 1950. (Very reliable and quite comprehensive.)